G000298649

INSIGHT INTO

BEREAVEMENT

CWR

INSIGHT INTO

BEREAVEMENT

Wendy Bray and Diana Priest

CWR

WAVERLEY ABBEY
INSIGHT SERIES

The *Waverley Abbey Insight Series* has been developed in response to the great need to help people understand and face some key issues that many of us struggle with today. CWR's ministry spans teaching, training and publishing, and this series draws on all of these areas of ministry.

Sourced from material first presented over Insight Days by CWR at their base, Waverley Abbey House, presenters and authors have worked in close co-operation to bring this series together, offering clear insight, teaching and help on a broad range of subjects and issues. Bringing biblical understanding and Godly insight, these books are written both for those who help others and those who face these issues themselves.

CONTENTS

FOREWORD

As I write this Foreword, I am reminded of a recent major item of news concerning a tragedy in Kentucky, USA, where the families of twelve coal miners were mistakenly told, after many long anxious hours of waiting and praying, that their loved ones had miraculously survived a pit disaster, only to be told an hour later that, in fact, only one had survived, with critical injuries, while the rest had perished. It's hard to imagine the agony of their experience as gratitude, relief and jubilation turned to shock, anger and the bitterness of grief. This is a dramatic example, and few, mercifully, will have such an experience to endure, yet we must all, in some way and at some time, face up to the truth that life involves loss and that the pain of bereavement is a fact of human existence.

My own long experience as a pastor and a counsellor powerfully suggests to me that many people are ill-prepared and ill-equipped to face the reality of loss, whether it be loss of a loved one, a job, a marriage, a lifestyle or a hope. Their philosophy or worldview simply does not readily enable them to weather the storm without damage. Similarly, while there may be real concern and compassion, there is often a deficit of understanding on the part of those who stand alongside seeking to help and support. This is a book to meet all of these needs as, for all its simplicity and straightforwardness of style, it is both deep and comprehensive. It is written with great honesty, and sometimes humour, drawing upon personal experiences of bereavement as well as many years of counselling and teaching others to counsel. It is also written from the perspective of someone deeply rooted in the Christian faith whose counsel is soundly based on and enriched by Scripture. The authors never lose sight of the book's twofold aim: to provide care and comfort through appropriate bereavement support *and* to help people find and experience God's love in the midst of loss.

As one whose personal bereavement journey has involved the loss of a beloved wife and sons and, in recent years, of health, strength and certain hopes and dreams, I commend this book as a resource offering insight, comfort, encouragement and a challenge to spiritual growth. While helpful to those seeking to develop professional or pastoral skills, and to those personally suffering loss, it deserves a place on the bookshelf of any men or women who seek a deeper understanding of themselves, of others and of God.

Selwyn Hughes
December 2005

INTRODUCTION

This booklet grew out of an Insight into Bereavement workshop held at Waverley Abbey House as part of CWR's pastoral training ministry.

It stems largely from the work and direction of Diana Priest, who led that seminar and whose words, experience and wisdom form its basis.

Diana has graciously allowed me to give the content of that day context for this book, and to fill the 'gaps' that inevitably appear when a live and interactive event takes place.

What is included here is designed to offer some insight and support to those who in turn wish to support others facing bereavement and loss, as well as for those who are themselves bereaved. It is not intended to be an authoritative work or a comprehensive manual exploring the journey of grief – we offer pointers to the work of others who have moved closer to that end. Rather, as 'insight' implies, it offers a personal perspective on the experience of bereavement, suggests ways of understanding that experience and offers practical ideas to meet the needs of the bereaved.

Its starting point is the necessary recognition that a wide range of different experiences of loss can leave us standing at the start of a bereavement journey. Loss may involve the traumatic death of a loved one, the end of a marriage, the stillbirth of a longed-for child, the loss of home or livelihood.

Each of those journeys will follow a similar bereavement pathway and share recognisable landmarks of loss, disbelief, grief and adaptation. But there is hope. Hope in the love offered by others and in the eternal hope promised by God. Even, if we look closely, hope in the suffering itself.

Because this book is designed for those who will help the bereaved as well as the bereaved themselves, it includes a process of self-reflection – something that is vital if those who care are to support others effectively. It is grounded in biblical truth and wrapped around with prayer.

Acknowledgement
I am indebted to Pablo Martinez and Ali Hull whose book *Tracing the Rainbow*[1] provided excellent background reading in the researching and writing of this book.

Wendy Bray

Note from Diana Priest

I have had a number of losses in my life: first losing my father when I was seven, then when I was fifty-two my husband died, after quite a time of suffering and the family loss in his redundancy.

I believe I have experienced most of the ranges of emotion connected with loss, and while not being able to identify with all in loss, I am nevertheless able to empathise to a large degree from my own experience and training as a nurse and counsellor. I do not pretend to know all about it, as grieving is unique to each person and circumstance, and carers need to be able to discern how each individual is experiencing loss from whatever cause.

I started leading bereavement seminars about twenty or more years ago and would like to acknowledge the late Selwyn Hughes and Shelley Fergusson for their part in the development of the material.

For further reading I would particularly like to recommend *Grief Counselling and Grief Therapy* by J. William Worden.

CHAPTER ONE

WHAT IS DEATH?

We begin with the most inevitable and all-encompassing of losses – death.

But as we do, we remind ourselves to fix our eyes on God:

O Lord, you are my God; I will exalt you and praise your name, for in perfect faithfulness you have done marvellous things, things planned long ago. You have made the city a heap of rubble, the fortified town a ruin, the foreigners' stronghold a city no more; it will never be rebuilt. Therefore strong peoples will honour you; cities of ruthless nations will revere you. You have been a refuge for the poor, a refuge for the needy in his distress, a shelter from the storm and a shade from the heat. For the breath of the ruthless is like a storm driving against a wall and like the heat of the desert. You silence the uproar of foreigners; as heat is reduced by the shadow of a cloud, so the song of the ruthless is stilled.

On this mountain the Lord Almighty will prepare a feast of rich food for all peoples, a banquet of aged wine – the best of meats and the finest of wines. On this mountain he will destroy the shroud that enfolds all peoples, the sheet that covers all nations; he will swallow up death for ever. The Sovereign LORD will wipe away the tears from all faces; he will remove the disgrace of his people from all the earth. The LORD has spoken.

In that day they will say, 'Surely this is our God; we trusted in him, and he saved us. This is the LORD, we trusted in him; let us rejoice and be glad in his salvation.' (Isa. 25:1–9)

Those words give us a sure and certain focus for an exploration of the most overwhelming of human experiences – loss and bereavement through death.

They remind us that even when our world is apparently crumbling and we are in the midst of devastation and bewilderment, God will not leave us or forsake us. He can be trusted.

WHAT IS DEATH?

A biblical and cultural perspective
Death is not easy to define. Our understanding of what it means both medically and spiritually has, in some senses, evolved with our understanding of life. It is also given a personal context of understanding through the experience of death we have each had in our own lives.

As our understanding of death has grown as a society, our definitions have assumed that when heart and life support systems stop functioning, death has occurred. Death is now measured for legal purposes in terms of brain activity and the sustainability of life. But 'death' may also be used simply to explain that someone has stopped breathing.

How we respond to death as individuals will depend to a large extent on the experience of death we have had in our own lives: from the way we were taught about death as children, to the way we have grieved as adults.

But what does the Bible say about death?

Biblically, Elijah raised the widow's son by breathing into him (1 Kings 17:17–22).

When speaking of death, the Bible uses the expression 'sleeping' (1 Cor. 15:20), a metaphor used much by the Victorians and as 'spiritual separation' (James 2:26) as at Jesus' death (John 19:30) when he 'gave up his spirit'.

The Bible also represents death as the result of sin; as the opposite of God-given life, and – in the case of natural death – as the end of life in the present world. The Bible teaches that life is fleeting (Psa. 90) and death is inevitable (Matt. 4:16; Heb. 9:27), although God designed death to be the inevitable result of sin rather than of life (Gen. 2:17).

What happens at that moment of death is a mystery. What little insight the Bible gives is hinted at in the story of the Rich Man and Lazarus (Luke 16:19–31) and Jesus' conversation with the thief on the cross (Luke 23:43). Both accounts give us an indication of what happens at the point of death if we live our life with – and without – Christ.

Life and death is presented as a dilemma for those who love Christ. It was certainly a dilemma for Paul as he struggled with wanting to live, yet longed to be with Christ (Phil. 1:21–23). He recognised the way in which death will be liberating for us as our bodies are 'redeemed' (Rom. 8:23).

As Christians, we have nothing to fear in death because we know that Jesus is beyond death and that we will be with

Him (Luke 23:43). Ultimately, He has the victory over sin and death and offers us a share in that victory through faith (John 11:25–26) so that not even death will separate us from His love (Rom. 8:37–39). What a wonderful assurance!

From a historical cultural perspective, the Greeks viewed death merely as the end of living. They had no philosophy of creation or death. There was no question of 'Why?' – theirs was a fatalistic view.

The Egyptians did believe in an afterlife and were required to give an account of their good and bad deeds to secure it. It was a philosophy which originated in the myths and legend of the gods and was an afterlife which seemed reserved for the pharaohs and those in high places. Uncovered tombs filled with possessions teach us that the Egyptians considered it necessary to take all their material possessions with them so that they would be well provided for in the afterlife.

In Christian society, views of death and associated rituals have changed much over the centuries, removing themselves from both Paul's perspective and Jesus' assurance.

Some cultures paid for 'professional' mourners in an approach to death that continued, to some extent, into the Victorian age when death was almost glorified. Much eighteenth- and nineteenth-century poetry and art reflects that view. It is imbued with an exaggerated sense of pathos, emphasising the supposed 'nobility' of grief and the prominence of the melodramatic.

The two World Wars gave a different and changing perspective. The First World War, the horrors of the trenches, and loss on a scale never seen before, meant that while death was still strangely glorified, stoicism ruled. There was little talk of grief or mourning.

It was 'one of those things', tolerated because it was for the common good; we were 'fighting for our country' and sending 'heroes' to the Front. The perspective of those who had witnessed such death and chronicled it was often rejected in favour of pro-war propaganda.

It was only well into, and beyond, the Second World War, that families began to be reluctant to encourage their young men to fight as they revisited the grief and loss they themselves had encountered. But there was still a reluctance to talk. Bereavement was private and personal. It often led to denial and a desensitisation of loss: it was endured, but never spoken of. Struggle was for the men at the Front, not the families left behind. There was and often still is a silence, an awkwardness and a withdrawal in the face of loss.

A growing interest in popular psychology, the accessibility of prominent lives and deaths through the media, and most particularly, the death of Diana, Princess of Wales, have changed the climate for the expression of and acceptability of grief. That event released something in our national community which gave permission for grief and tears and an acknowledged sense of loss. As a result, it is now much more permissible to talk about loss and grief. That 'national' time of mourning initiated and developed personal thought and wider discussion and has left us with much more of an awareness of what grief is all about. It has led to people being willing, if they are struggling with loss, to seek specialist support and counselling.

The work of Kubler-Ross, Dame Cecily Saunders and others, means that we are now much more aware of caring for the dying. The hospice movement is more widely understood and supported and we are prioritising the needs both of those approaching death and of those who grieve.

Exploring aspects of bereavement and loss, grief and dying, must always include consideration of, and preparation for, anticipated loss and grief.

Our view of death is affected by our values and beliefs about it. A humanist approach will be very different from that of a believing Christian and even for Christians there will be questions that we need to acknowledge and face. Beyond those questions, Christians do have a hope of eternal life and we can hold on to that with certainty (1 Pet. 1:3).

What do we learn about death from Jesus' attitude to it?

Jesus knew that He had victory over death – and He knew that we could have that victory. But His attitude in the face of death was still one of empathy and compassion. He wept with those who wept and He shared their grief (John 11:35).

He responded to the grief of a father for his daughter, yet as He looked at that daughter He said that she was not dead but 'asleep' (Mark 5:39), indicating that physical death is not final.

Even while dying on the cross, He heard the trusting words of the thief hanging to one side of Him and reassured him that, 'Today you will be with me in paradise' (Luke 23:43). He knew the heart of that man and saw his faith. In His compassion He gave assurance of life beyond death.

There is something overriding and marvellous in that statement: 'You will be with me.' It speaks of security, resolution, hope. We may not completely understand the theology, but we can take comfort from the fact that those are the words of Jesus – even as He suffered and died. We don't have to fear death because our hope is for life eternal.

Jesus as the Christ had – and still has – victory over death. He had faith that He would rise again. He knew He would be with His Father. He was the very first to have victory over death so that we could also know that powerful victory through faith. Jesus still knew fear and apprehension in the *face* of death, however. He asked for the 'cup' to be taken from Him and experienced separation from God (Matt. 26:36–42; 27:46).

But that separation was temporary, and through the darkness of the sacrifice it entailed burst the unbelievable grace-filled love of the Father.

Death is not the end for Christians. But the Bible tells us plainly that for the unbeliever there is a second death (Rev. 2:11). We cannot escape that fact – but we can share our hope.

For others, there will be a fear of death which has almost been 'taught'.

Diana tells the story of her grandmother, who, just before she died, said to her granddaughter: 'You know, life is sweet, Diana, whatever age you are.' Diana says:

> She was frightened of death. She had no assurance and she went to her grave fearing what would be on the other side. She was the result of a Victorian upbringing in which death was a weapon. Hell and Hades were used as a threat to 'make little girls be good'. There was no looking towards the victory that is beyond death.

Coming to, or bringing people to, a place of at least questioning a personal position in the face of death, is one of the approaches that might be used to explore the whole experience of loss and grief. That 'place' which needs exploration may not be in the experience of one who is dying, or even of one who is grieving, but of the one who is supporting them. In the experience of the loss of another, we are all faced with our own loss and our own mortality.

Diana shares that when her husband died at the age of fifty-five many people in her church family mentioned that they had never really thought about their own mortality. Her husband's death had made them stop and think. They became willing and able to talk about their faith in the face of another's death.

How much more do we need to give space for those who do not claim any faith to explore those issues?

Ultimately we have to put our trust in a God of mercy and grace, who knows our hearts and the hearts of those who die without, apparently, knowing Him.

What does the Bible say about the meaning of death?

The Bible asks us to view death as a bridge to something better. It reminds us that our times are in God's hands (Psa. 31:15). Each of us has an appointment with death – but it is not the end. We will leave this worn-out, diseased body and be given a new physical form. Not a floppy, see-through spiritual cloak, but a strong and healthy body in which to enjoy life in all its fullness.

Wendy has a friend whose body has been ravaged by a lifetime of illness. She clings almost daily to that promise of a new body that is fit and healthy and able to move and breathe without restriction, weakness or pain. It is part of her 'hope'.

Writer and speaker Joni Eareckson Tada has a similar hope. A quadriplegic since a diving accident in her teens, she tells of how she has dreamt of a tanned and strong body beyond death with which she will swim again, without fear and with great enthusiasm.

We do not know exactly what will happen beyond death. We know that we will stand before Jesus and will give some account of ourselves to Him. But we also know that we will do so in security and love and not in shame, because we are saved by grace. There is no condemnation (Rom. 8:1–2) for those who love Jesus.

The Bible gives considerable emphasis to the loss of relationship – however temporary – that death results in. And, of course, that is exactly what those who are grieving will give most importance to. It is the loss of relationship in life, of closeness, intimacy and familiarity that they mourn.

Death, in a biblical sense, is separation from the life that a relationship with God – with its model for that closeness, intimacy and familiarity – gives us. We have inherited that separation from Adam and Eve who turned their back on what God had ordained as relationship and chose sin and death. With that separation we have inherited death and decay. There was only one way to know an end to that separation. Jesus needed to share it: to taste death for us. In Gethsemane, He knew a genuine fear of separation from His Father, however temporary (Matt. 26:36–42).

It follows that we too will be frightened of the actual point of death and what it may involve. But our faith carries us to, through and beyond the realities of life *and* death. Daniel and his friends (Dan. 3) demonstrated a faith which faced those realities when they said, 'the God we serve is able to save us' (Dan. 3:17) and then, 'But even if he does not …' (v.18). They were aware that their God might choose not to save them on that occasion, but their faith in God's goodness remained. They knew that God would have the victory in death or life, flames or not.

That is the Christian's victory over death. Even if we die, God is still there for us. He still has the victory – the ultimate victory.

Thousands of Christian martyrs have died with those words of faith on their lips.

PERSONAL REFLECTION

Looking at our own histories of loss helps us to enter into the world of those suffering loss and grief. Take some time out to complete the statements below. You may not need, or be able, to answer every one, but reflecting on your own experience will help you as you seek to empathise with the grief of others.

1. The first death I can remember was the death of …
2. I was age …
3. The feelings I remember I had at the time were …
4. The first funeral (wake or other ritual) I ever attended was for …
5. I was age …
6. The thing I most remember about the experience is …
7. My most recent loss by death was … (person, time, circumstances)
8. I coped with this loss by …
9. The most difficult loss for me was the death of …
10. It was difficult because …
11. Of the important people in my life who are now living, the most difficult death would be the death of …
12. It would be the most difficult because …
13. My primary style of coping with loss is …
14. I know my own grief is resolved when …
15. It is appropriate for me to share my own experiences of grief with a client when …

From *Grief Counselling and Grief Therapy*, J. William Worden.

PRAYER
Father, as we contemplate death – remind us that we have life. Amen.

CHAPTER TWO

WHAT IS BEREAVEMENT AND LOSS?

Bereavement is to be robbed of something, to be dispossessed, usually of immaterial things like life and hope. It is to be left desolate and deprived. For our purposes – the bereavement of a relationship – *Vine's Expository Dictionary* gives the Greek word for bereaved as *aporphanizomai* – 'orphan'.

Loss is the act, the instance or the privation resulting from that bereavement. Grief, by comparison, is deep or violent sorrow, a keen regret, the Greek word for which is *lupe* signifying pain of body or mind. Grief is both a process and a feeling.

Grief is the other side of love, even *part* of love. It is the risk we take in loving fully and long. Gerald Sittser writes movingly:

Loss creates a barren present, as if one were sailing on a vast sea of nothingness. Those who suffer loss live life suspended between a sea of past for which they long and a future for which they hope. They want to return to the harbour of the familiar past and recover what was lost ... Or they want to sail on and discover a meaningful future that promises to bring them life again ... instead they find themselves living in a barren present that is empty of meaning.[1]

Bereavement, loss and grief can be caused by anything that constitutes *change*: change involving any part of our world or existence, even our hopes and dreams – and it often has much to do with our sense of identity.

We each react to any kind of loss in ways that are uniquely personal. There are generalities and universalities in the experience – but each individual's experience of loss will be unique. In each situation grieving and bereavement will follow. When two have been one, separation is like being torn apart. The longer a marriage has been enjoyed, the harder that tearing apart can be – through death or divorce.

Anne and her husband Tony were very close. Theirs was a 'hand-in-glove' relationship. Anne depended on Tony utterly. Then Tony died in an accident while abroad on business. They had lived their lives so much entwined, that losing Tony was like that glove being ripped off the hand. Anne was emotionally raw, her suffering prolonged as her grief became complicated. Establishing the details of the death was a difficult process and it was years before Anne felt able to visit the place where Tony had died and know some kind of closure. The very closeness and joy they had experienced made the separation and bereavement process much more difficult.

Older couples especially often live and work together in tandem from the point of retirement. They may drive, cook or shop in such partnership that losing the other is like losing part of their very self. Co-dependence often results in a loss of identity, a feeling that this or that job can no longer be done without the other. Part of that identity is lost as a role is ended.

A mother may lose her only child and so her role as a mother; a son his role as 'son' on the death of his surviving parent. A divorced woman may feel heavily the loss of her role as 'wife', however difficult that role may lately have been. With the loss of a partner, a son or daughter, not only will a unique relationship be lost but the very name – the identification – of that relationship.

Untimely or unexpected death – miscarriage, stillbirth, suicide, accident or murder – brings with it a greater element of shock and misplacement. It often means a change in lifestyle and life perspective and a sense that things are not as they should be – even that a 'mistake' has been made. That response may often lead into a more complicated grieving process.

Other types of loss

Loss in any form leads to a degree of bereavement and grief.

- *Divorce and separation – loss of love*

Marital breakdown produces grief which is partnered by anger, hurt and bitterness. When someone dies, however ill the person may have been or however difficult the relationship, a line can at least, however painfully, be drawn. Divorce and separation is not final. There is an 'afterlife': a recurring battle, a seeping bitterness or a clinging on to hope which is rarely fulfilled.

Divorce affects not just the separating partners and their children but wider family and community, who all experience a degree of loss. Divorce is a public loss. The grieving process follows a similar pattern to that which follows death, but with some distinct differences.

Unlike the pain involved in the death of a partner, the pain of the divorced is (generally) caused by the one who is lost – and usually deliberately. Anger and betrayal are central emotions. There is always an element of blame in divorce – a sense of guilt and personal failure are part of that.

Nobody is prepared for divorce – we all hope our marriages will last. Neither do we have an opportunity to learn how to grieve in a divorce situation. The result can be a sense of overwhelming loss, confusion, doubt and often unanswerable – even unaskable questions.

Because divorce does not mean a 'clean break' after loss it can gather complications in its wake. Continuing to see the person who is lost – perhaps because of the children – rubs salt in the wounds: especially if they are happily living a new life with a new partner. That clean break would so often be so much easier to bear.

All too often, the divorced find themselves marginalised in the very place that should hold them and their pain close – the church. Their need is for someone to be there – without judgment – as they experience the pain of loss of relationship. Jesus was there. He was there – without condemnation – with the woman caught in adultery. He was there with all those who found themselves in the margins. Those that care need to be there standing in the margins, looking out for the losses and holding close the lost.

- *Trauma – loss of security*
Injury after an accident or personal attack shakes not only physical well-being but emotional stability. Confidence in the outside world is lost and the ability to remain safe is questioned. Loss of virginity or self-image through rape or assault has

long-term implications which need skilled specialist counselling and support.

Trauma of any kind includes a devastating sense of loss, and post-traumatic stress syndrome affects even those trained to deal with trauma, such as paramedics and firefighters.

The question, 'Could I have done something?' remains.

- *Multiple losses*

Sometimes, one loss will lead to multiple losses.

Rosemary had worked abroad with her husband as part of a mission team for thirty years and her children had grown up amidst its distinct culture. When her husband died she was required to return home to the UK – which wasn't 'home' at all. The mission organisation could no longer support her and was closing down its operations. She returned to what was, to Rosemary and the youngest child who returned with her, an alien culture. She had little money, no home and had left her remaining family in the country where she had spent most of her adult life, all of which complicated a loss that on its own would have been traumatic. Her losses included not only several family members – through death and separation, but friends, home, country and livelihood: her very identity.

- *Subtle and 'invisible' losses*

It is often the subtle and unexpected losses that are the hardest to bear. Some losses are even invisible. A woman unable to conceive cannot share her desperation with keen grandparents who ask 'When will it be you?'

Somebody who is very poor may know a form of grieving when they see other people who have plenty.

'Empty Nest Syndrome' is very real, especially for parents who have lived much of their life for their children or who depend upon them for love, worth or status. A quiet house and a 'too tidy bedroom' can make a heart ache.

- *Unemployment – loss of a livelihood*

Losing employment leads not only to the loss of a job and financial security but dignity, and a sense of self-worth. If a man or woman has seen him or herself as breadwinner there can be a sense of shame and helplessness in being unable to provide for their family.

So much of our self-worth is tied up with our job or professional standing that losing it can be like losing part of our very self.

Gary lost his job with an insurance firm but still continued to leave home at the same time each day, unable to face telling his wife. It wasn't until more than a week later that he was able to confess. And only then because of their coincidental meeting in the local library where Gary had been spending a large part of his day.

- *Loss of hope*

When all that was planned for doesn't happen, dreams are shattered and longings face disappointment, there is a loss of hope. Failed exams, a house move that 'falls through', a job that didn't materialise are all part of the ups and downs of life. But they can be very real losses nonetheless. A broken engagement may mean loss of dreams for a 'together' future: a loss of what might have been. An unexpected hysterectomy or loss of fertility may signal the final loss of the dream of being a mother. Very real bereavement can follow.

Regrets can also be tangled with loss. All of us will hold memories of 'If only' in our hearts. Those 'If onlys' are personal and relative: what might be a fleeting regret to one person may have a major impact on the life of another.

- *Loss of health*

Illness means a loss of health – albeit temporarily – and long-term illness can mean that the whole prospect of the life that had been planned and imagined is now changed. Plans need to be redrawn. Not just for the one who is ill but for the family and friends supporting them. The waiting involved in long-term illness can also be a place of grief as 'normal life' is lost and the prospect of its return is delayed.

- *Body image*

Chemotherapy or surgery may lead to a loss of hair or breast. An accident may result in the loss of a limb or mobility or result in scarring. Both will lead to loss of looks and an essence of acceptability in the eyes of others. Disability means the loss of freedom and independence; even the loss of choice. Ageing causes many people to experience a genuine mourning of the loss of body image, fitness or mental faculty as they grow older.

Loss and identity

Bereavement and loss carry with them the question 'Who am I?' Loss demands a readjustment of position, a re-evaluation of who we are and what we value in the light of what we have lost: Have I become (if I am married or in a long-term relationship) part of the identity of both the people in that relationship? Who am I without that relationship?

31

The degree of loss might depend on how important that status has become. The mother who can't let go of her children when they leave home because she no longer feels needed will suffer much more than the one who recognises that part of her role has come to a natural end. She will have been anticipating that end, even relishing the thought that they have reached adulthood safely – and at last she will have some time to herself! Most will be somewhere between the two, but will often swing painfully between poles.

Redundancy through loss of a paid job can bring multiple identity losses: of job title, status and authority as well as role of breadwinner. The loss of that job, of a position of authority or a community role may mean ceasing to be viewed as a leader or as an influential member of the workforce or community. There is kudos, a security, a worth in the role that is lost. Even when loss is chosen – giving up work to stay at home with children, for example – there may still be the sense of loss of status and identity or the need to develop a new identity to fit the new role.

Loss is very rarely just what it seems from the outside. The internal effects are often hidden, complex and far-reaching. Those who are bereaved may need to be helped to voice their sense of loss and move – in their own time and healing – beyond it.

Grief is an experience characterised by emptiness and by waiting, and waiting is hard. If we are carers, we may not be able to fill the emptiness but we can wait with the one who feels so very empty.

EFFECTS OF LOSS AND BEREAVEMENT

Loss will be felt not just emotionally – but also physically and socially. Mary, who worked in Africa for many years, uses a beautiful analogy of loss which illustrates the fragility of our emotions. She explains that when she arrived back from Africa after fourteen years, adjusting to the UK was difficult: 'I felt a bit like a dandelion clock, all the bits of me were blown and scattered everywhere.' The bereaved will often describe their loss in a similar way, as feeling as if they have been broken into pieces. They don't know where to put those pieces – even if they can be gathered – and they will probably never be put back in the same places again.

They will eventually find places for those lost or broken pieces – it might even be a better arrangement. But it will take time for the fragments to settle and 'fit' once more.

The manifestations and effects of loss

Physical responses to loss and bereavement can be closely linked to emotions. Or they may simply be a manifestation of the shock and trauma that has been faced.

• *Confusion*

The bereaved person may experience memory loss and a sense of imbalance. Simple things can become enormously complicated.

Selwyn Hughes relayed an incident that occurred in the early days following the death of his wife which illustrates that confusion well.

He drove to fill the car up with petrol at a local petrol station, but found that he couldn't remember how to do it. A simple task he had performed innumerable times before became a challenge.

He had driven to the garage, but the process and routine of filling the car with petrol escaped him.

- *Tears*

Weeping is a healthy and often necessary response to grief. Not everyone will cry – or need to cry. It is perfectly possible for someone to grieve without tears and they shouldn't be coerced. The Bible asks us to weep with those who weep (Rom. 12:15, NKJV), not force them to do so!

But most will find relief and release in tears in private and public. Learning to weep without shame is an important step in the grieving process, and one which moves the bereaved forward on their bereavement journey. Being given permission, space and a safe place to cry as much as is needed can be liberating – and healing.

God feels the sorrow of our tears – He even counts them ('You have stored my tears … and counted each of them', Psa. 56:8, CEV) but He promises healing (see, for example, 2 Kings 20:5). Tears shed on earth will be shared in heaven.

- *Yearnings and imaginings*

Often a bereaved person will believe that they have seen the person who has died or heard their voice. This doesn't mean the bereaved is 'losing it' or getting into the spiritualist realms! The mind tells us to expect what it has always seen. Our physiology has been traumatised, our logic turned on its head, and as a result, our mind inadvertently tells us lies.

The experience of someone who says, 'I'm sure he was here last night, I could feel his presence' or 'I could hear him' should not be dismissed, minimised or challenged – but accepted. It will pass or be more generally assimilated into their experience in time.

Shortly after bereavement, it is easy for a wife who has lost her husband to hear a door bang and be sure he is returning – even to the extent of actually hearing a voice. Auditory hallucinations are not something to worry about in the early stages of bereavement. The mind is merely saying, 'I have always heard that voice; why wouldn't I hear it now?' So it does.

- *The need for small steps*

When the physical and mental effort of the day is overwhelming, it can help to focus on detail. If the bereaved person is able to cope with the tiny bits of a day, they will cope longer term. Having control over a small piece of life – making a cup of tea – reminds them that they are not falling apart: 'I can actually make a cup of tea!' It doesn't help when someone else – however caring – does everything for them. Small steps of independence and control will lead to longer strides.

- *Mood swings*

Bereavement causes the pendulum in our emotional clock to lose its momentum. It is as if someone has turned the clock case upside down and shaken it. As a result the pendulum swings in all directions unexpectedly in anxiety and despair. Whether the bereaved is widowed, separated or divorced, emotions can veer between hate and anger, love and yearning, strong rejection and a desire to reunite.

One young woman, whose husband had recently left, wrote that on one day she might be 'afraid to see him because I fear I will want to hold him' while on another she wanted to 'lash out at his chest' in anger.

- *A sense of failure*

Diminished self-esteem causes the separated and divorced to ask, 'Wasn't I good enough?' 'What did I do?' in an atmosphere of self-reproach and bewilderment. This is especially the case when the partner left behind had not foreseen any problems, or believed the relationship to be happy.

- *Sleeplessness and overwhelming tiredness*

Being tired after bereavement is no guarantee of sleep. Short-term medication may help, although natural rhythms will return eventually without medication, and disruption of life's order for a while should not be criticised. But the night can be a lonely place. Having someone to 'stay over' when a person is very recently bereaved can help, especially if the visitor is also prepared to get up at 3am to make tea and chat! But it should be a temporary or even a one-off event to avoid dependency.

Normal sleep patterns will generally return in time, although some people will never sleep in quite the same way again without their partners.

- *Panic attacks*

Confusion and disorientation may lead to panic attacks while in a public place.

Emotions can often overwhelm by surprise and render the bereaved person physically incapable of the simplest tasks: finishing the shopping, boarding the bus, entering the post office.

Having company to do the simple chores for a while until confidence returns, will help. But we should not be tempted to take over or the bereaved may start to feel incapable and not worthy of respect.

- *Idealising*

A tendency to idealise the dead person can go on for some time. When we are bereaved, we won't want to acknowledge the difficult times, or the negative sides to the personality of the one we are missing – even when talking to those who knew them. We may continue to say: 'Jack would do that' or 'Joan would never have gone there' even if that isn't the case. It is a way of keeping that person and their influence alive and of cherishing their memory. The closer people are to each other the more this is likely to happen. This often happens for older people who have lived 'hand-in-glove'.

- *A sense of social exclusion*

The bereaved often feel as if they don't 'fit' into the world of couples, happy families or ordinary life.

In the film *Calendar Girls* Annie, played by actress Julie Walters, has recently lost her husband John to leukaemia. When the WI calendar produced to raise funds for the local hospital becomes something of a sensation, Annie finds herself unable to join in with the partying involved in the publicity – even in the salubrious surroundings of a swanky LA hotel. Her first need is to write to the many families similarly bereaved, and she is pictured shut away in her hotel room, surrounded by letters, immune to the celebratory atmosphere – almost as if in another world.

As Margaret left the hospital after the death of her mother, she genuinely could not understand why the world as she knew it hadn't stopped. She wondered why shops were still open, birds were singing, cars were driving along the street and people were continuing to chat and laugh as they stood on pavements.

The sense of being a social outcast is common. C.S. Lewis in *A Grief Observed* writes:

> An odd by-product of my loss is that I am aware of being an embarrassment to everybody I meet, at work, at the Club, in the street. I see people as they approach me trying to make up their minds whether they will say something about it or not. I hate it if they do and if they don't ... perhaps the bereaved ought to be isolated in special settlements like lepers.[2]

- *After-effects of divorce*

Physical symptoms may express grief. After divorce it is common to witness compulsive eating or extreme weight loss, menstrual disorders, rashes and hair loss in the one who is grieving. Psychosomatic illness often masks emotional pain.

Even those who welcome separation and loss to the extent of celebrating their divorce face the effects of bereavement at some point: a song from 'happier times' can trigger recognition of loss of what might have been or what had been hoped for, a reminder that the love once longed for has been lost.

We will explore the *process* that carries the effects of loss in more detail in later chapters. At this point, the key thing to remember is that everyone's experience of loss and bereavement is different. We should never be surprised by behaviour, or make assumptions about response. In the early stages that response may even be bizarre – but nothing is 'wrong' or 'bad'. It is up to carers to be part of something, rather like a three-legged challenge: to be another leg for a person for a while; to help the one who has been bereaved through the assault course that is bereavement and out the other side. That challenge involves accepting the bereaved person and sticking close (however bumpy and uneven their stride, whatever the obstacle, whichever direction they want to pull in and however slow the progress) but not making them move before they are ready.

EMOTIONS CONNECTED TO LOSS

Emotions are paramount in any experience of loss. Whilst we have not space to consider each in turn, we will consider their part in the bereavement journey in the next chapter. For now we need to be aware that we may feel or witness any combination of ...

- Unbelief
- Panic
- Guilt
- Sadness
- Anger
- Remorse
- Self-reproach
- Vengeance
- Mood swings
- Fear
- Regret
- Frustration
- Questioning
- Wondering
- Pain
- Bitterness

- Relief
- Denial
- Numbness

… and probably more besides.

Emotions work in partnership together or hide one another in bereavement. They become tangled and difficult to distinguish, like a ball of wool that has been tossed around by a kitten. It may be part of the role of the companion in grief and loss to identify the strands and help untie the knots.

PERSONAL REFLECTION

- If you have suffered loss what were some of the feelings you experienced? Use the list above to help you identify the emotions behind them.
- Ask God to help you to understand or acknowledge/re-acknowledge each feeling in turn and ensure your healing within it.
- How might your experience of loss and your understanding of your own feelings help you to stand alongside another who is grieving?

PRAYER
Father, use my pain and healing to help me share the pain and see the healing of another. Amen.

CHAPTER THREE

THE BEREAVEMENT JOURNEY

Grief is unique to each bereaved person. But there is some universality of experience. The journey is taken via many different routes with some shared scenery and with each traveller arriving at different points at different times, even in a different order. No bereavement journey is too long or too short, but some may be complicated, subject to delay and filled with images and experiences that will have life-long impact.

Grief is also hard work. It is slow, demanding, exhausting work that stretches our emotional muscles. It also involves repetitive, often lonely tasks.

Bereavement, then, is a 'working' journey. It is not a linear process with a definite beginning and end to each stage but, like the musical score accompanying a lament, it is an overlapping, ebbing and flowing composition.

From journey's start to journey's end the bereaved will be working at:

- Accepting the reality of their loss
- Experiencing pain
- Adjusting to life without the person who has died or been lost
- Withdrawing and then reinvesting in life with others

STAGES OF LOSS

Loss is experienced in three main stages which may overlap at any point.

- Disbelief and protest
- Despair
- Reorganisation and adjustment

Each stage impacts mind, body, emotions and spirituality.

Disbelief and protest

An emotional response to disbelief and shock will involve periods of anger, hurt, upset and fear. It may also include initial denial: a sense of saying 'No' with every part of the mind and body, or a numbness that leads to calm or a sense of unreality. As emotions shut down that numbness often provides a cushion from reality. Pain comes gradually as reality dawns and emotion flows – much like the blood flow after the shock of a cut. This is the point when help is most needed.

Stages of loss

Developed with Shelley Fergusson from material produced by CWR, Colin Murray Parkes, Elizabeth Kubler-Ross

PHASES	DISBELIEF / PROTEST	DESPAIR	RE-ORGANISATION / ADJUSTMENT
EMOTIONS The Heart	• Shock • Numbness • Calm/denial • Unreal	• Angry • Upset • Hurt • 'No' • Afraid	• Sadness and hopeless • Confusion • Yearning/longing • Emptiness, guilt, loss of meaning, poor self-esteem, pining, loneliness, vulnerable	• More hopeful • Calmer • Meaning regained • Accepting	• Emotions • Available for others
BEHAVIOUR The Mind	• 'Elsewhere' • Forgetful • Anxious • Searching	• Irritable • Argumentative • Blaming • Aggressive • Anxious	• Tearful • Loss of motivation • Depressed, withdrawn • Loss of confidence • Pre-occupation	• New skills and responsibilities • Confidence • Social changes	• New interests • New relationships
PHYSICAL EFFECTS The Body	• Feeling 'not there' • Tightness in throat and chest • Dry mouth • Easily startled • 'Butterflies'	• Churning stomach • Tense-aching • Agitated, fearful • Shortness of breath	• Bodily pain • Loss of appetite • Sighing • Sleep disturbance • Insomnia and dreams • Exhaustion • Illness and accidents	• More energy • Normal patterns of sleep/eating	• Increase in activities and outside life
SPIRITUAL IMPACT The Spirit	• Cushion from reality	• Angry with God • Unable to pray	• Faith irrelevant – empty – or sustaining	• Finding renewed meaning and relevance in spiritual terms • Life after death	• Letting go – growing
TASKS OF MOURNING	1. Accepting reality of loss	2. Experiencing Grief	3. Adjust to 'life without deceased'	4. Withdraw and re-invest

Characteristic behaviour might demonstrate:

- A sense of unreality, of not being in touch with the real world
- Anxiety
- Feeling lost, as if searching for something or someone in response to the loss
- Anger as irritability, argumentativeness, looking for someone or something to blame, bargaining, recklessness or aggression
- Fearful, nervous and agitated behaviour: pacing, wringing the hands
- Lack of confidence about simple tasks and routines

As thinking processes slow, the bereaved person may need very specific instructions in order to do tasks rather than generalities, for example, 'Open the cat food tin.' Not just, 'Feed the cat.'

There may be complicated paperwork or personal and financial affairs to work through which seem overwhelming. Those affairs may have been left in disarray, which will in itself cause hurt, even resentment.

The job of a carer may be to help to identify priorities for action – not taking over the tasks – enabling the bereaved to gain control of the bigger picture. That may require the assistance or engagement of professional services. Helping to find a reliable and trustworthy accountant or solicitor may be a vital detail of long-term support.

Physically, shock can produce tightness in the throat and chest, breathlessness or a dry mouth. 'Butterflies' or a churning stomach are common, as are tension aches and pains. Normal sleeping and eating patterns are lost and just 'existing' in the world demands incredible physical effort.

The spiritual or faith impact of this first stage may involve blaming God. But it can also result in an unreal 'super–spirituality' which is shocking in its apparent 'lessening' of the loss. Christians can believe, say and do all the 'right' things, apply Christian platitudes to their own suffering, but be cushioned from the reality by what they believe their 'faith-filled' response should be. It may take some time for reality to dawn, for permission to grieve to be accepted, to recognise that it is OK to acknowledge dark and difficult emotions before God –and even meet Him in them.

Janey organised and took centre stage of a lively thanksgiving service for her husband just days after his death. Her ebullience and 'triumphalism' were of great concern to friends and family – and short-lived. Janey entered a long period of complicated grief soon afterwards. It was as if she had fallen from a great height.

This first stage of the bereavement journey can continue for some time until the bereaved can 'let go' and abandon themselves to the next necessary stage of loss.

Despair

Despair engages the emotions utterly: sadness, hopelessness, confusion, yearning and longing fill long days and nights. Guilt is common, life loses meaning and hopelessness and poor self-esteem can pervade.

Emerging from shock and numbness can lead the bereaved into an attempt to find long-term understanding of their situation. Much of that understanding is sought through questions: 'What's the point?'; 'Where am I going from here?'; 'How can I go on without him/her?'

There can also be:

- a lack of confidence
- withdrawal
- a preoccupation with the dead person or his or her death
- excessive tearfulness
- loneliness
- depression

Understanding the degree of loss and the impact that loss will have in different areas of life can be helped by recognising just how central the person who has died was to the life of the one left behind. This is as much the case in situations of divorce and separation as in death.

It may also be helpful for the bereaved to list the smaller losses that the central bereavement has brought, in order to help uncover some of the depth of the loss experienced. Perhaps there is a loss of mobility because 'I never learnt to drive'; a loss of a sense of safety when 'I don't like being in the house alone at night'; a loss of financial security and sense of control because 'He did all that'. Identifying each loss and listing them can seem daunting, but it may eventually make it easier to face and handle each one and it will help to develop practical strategies first and emotional adaptation gradually.

Loneliness is not often directly expressed by the bereaved. Talkativeness and body language may give clues, but sometimes those grieving will reject others because they do not actually want to be seen in a state of grief. They feel vulnerable, so would almost 'prefer' to be lonely.

Often it is the simplest – and loveliest – things which usher in loneliness. Diana found that the loneliest time for her after the death of her husband was when she had finished gardening:

> I always used to look forward to my husband saying, 'Oh you've done a good job there, doesn't that look lovely!' That was the time I felt most lonely even though I had a lot of people around me. I couldn't have said I was a very lonely person, but those were lonely moments.

If carers are sensitive, they can spot the 'lonely moments'. Carers don't always need to say or do very much, just acknowledge that they have recognised the moment – perhaps by a touch of the arm, or by just saying something that indicates that they are there.

Joyce found it difficult to attend church after her husband's death. Not because she felt overwhelmed by the care given by other church members (as they assumed), but simply because she had always held John's hand throughout the sermon. Once he had died there were no hands to hold.

Louise found events at her son's school, carol concerts and Sports Day particularly hard to bear after her separation because her husband had always gone with her. She had never felt as lonely as in those 'crowds'. Her response was to co-ordinate a group of other lone parents who simply went together, making a social event of the time afterwards with the children in tow. Many new friendships resulted from that practical solution.

Behaviour that links the body and emotions may be unpredictable and tearfulness a constant companion during the despair stage (Psa. 42:3). But tears should never be discouraged. They really are a blessing, with healing properties that allow the release of emotions. The body and emotions often meet in grief with the occurrence of deep sighing. This involuntary response comes from the very depths and seems to communicate grief and sorrow that words cannot express.

Physical effects are often more apparent at this stage as the grief becomes 'chronic' and enters a 'long-term' stage. Hypochondriac tendencies can result when the bereaved person focuses on themselves and on their aches, pains and difficulties, particularly if they have suffered loss through illness. Illness can then become a focus for topics of conversation. Minor illness and accidents are also particularly common because self-care is not a priority and the mind is elsewhere.

The bereaved person may often lose motivation and confidence for day-to-day living, struggling to face alone those tasks that have always been done 'together'. A carer's response should not be to do those tasks for the one who is floundering, but to facilitate independence in the 'new' task, which in turn will build confidence and the recognition of an ability to cope and eventually to move forward.

Often there is a tendency for the bereaved to daydream or be preoccupied with aspects of the death, to find out details and dwell upon them, to wonder, 'If only'. Sleep disturbance, dreams and nightmares, insomnia and exhaustion are common. Nights can be long and lonely, and the bereaved person may dread going to bed or drifting off to sleep. Doing so may seem like another kind of loss – of control. They may dread the dark, the quiet, or the dreams and nightmares that plague them.

Beryl found that drifting off to sleep with the radio playing softly helped to fill the silence she so dreaded and Joyce moved her portable TV set into the bedroom for 'company'. 'A dreadful habit!' she claimed cheerfully later, having deterred her grand-children from doing the same! But the sight and sound of others 'nearby' before sleep and on waking helped her through the first difficult weeks.

Appetite may also be poor or lost completely and routines may drag or become confused.

When Wendy called to take Anne, who was recently bereaved, out to do essential shopping at 2pm, she found her still in her dressing gown. She had, quite simply, lost track of the time. Morning routines which would normally have been sped through had taken hours longer.

A faith response at this early stage may range from a feeling that faith is irrelevant or empty, to a clear knowledge of being sustained even against expectation: 'I can't explain it, but I just feel carried along.'

This initial period of despair may last some time. The elderly especially may live as though the death was yesterday for months, even years. Grief may then become more complicated and require specialist help.

However, most bereaved people will come through the despair stage in time and begin to rebuild their lives, adjusting to their loss. Some slight movement towards beginning to live life in a balanced way again will, hopefully, be evident.

Reorganisation and adjustment

Sometimes there will be movement between stages of the bereavement journey – like an ebb and flow – and the time taken to rebuild a balanced life will vary from person to person. There is no 'right' time. The diagram overleaf shows a 'wheel model' which explains this process in terms of crossing from one side of the wheel to the other before finally spinning off to reorganise or

Grief Cycle

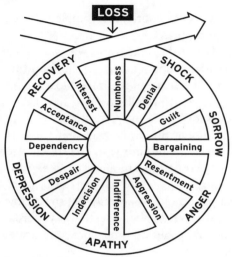

rebuild life. Grieving people must be reassured that each stage is normal, and that they are not, as they often express, 'going mad'. They will, in time, move on. Life will become closer to the 'normal' they knew before, even if it is lacking the person who helped to make it so.

Penelope Lively, who has often written movingly of the experience of grief in her novels, expresses the effect of gradual adjustment to loss powerfully in her novel *Perfect Happiness*:

Loss clamped her every morning as she woke. It sat its grinding weight on her and rode her, like the old man of the sea. It roared in her ears when people talked to her so that frequently she did not hear what they said. It interrupted her when she spoke so that she faltered in mid-sentence, lost track. A little less now remissions came and went. The days stalked by, taking her with them.[1]

As those days 'stalk by' it is often those on the outside of the grieving experience who have expectations that can't be met. After six months or so they assume that the grieving friend or relative should be 'over it' by now. They want closure.

For the one who still grieves, caring appears to have ceased, invitations stop, company drifts away and there is pressure to be 'OK'. Friends say, 'You should be pulling yourself together by now'; 'It's time to start living again' and then wonder why there are still tears and why the bereaved person still needs to talk about the person they have lost. Very often the bereaved will need to talk *more* at this stage. There is a need to tap into memories – anniversaries and birthdays – and give them significance. Caring needs to go on in different ways in response; there is still grieving work to be done.

We need to remember the social implications of loss. For many people, loneliness will get worse. They remember the one who has died and feel that 'there will never be anyone else like them'. In response they may cut themselves off from the outside world, only to compound the problem. The loneliness they feel then becomes loneliness without anybody rather than just without the person they have lost.

At these later stages of grief, one of the most helpful things to be encouraged is the development of friendships – old and new – so that the bereaved person has a number of people to do things with, and alongside. Individual carers need to ensure that they are not the 'only' friend.

Adjustment and divorce

Marks of adjustment specific to divorce can be identified as a sign that the divorcee is moving on.

They will:

- Be more able to face the demands of day-to-day life
- Begin to face life without their former partner in a more realistic and honest way
- Be more able to control their anger and hostility – however it is displayed
- Grasp – and give – a rational and reasonable explanation of how the marriage broke down without assigning undue blame and recognising weaknesses and strengths
- Acknowledge that the process of recovery will take time
- Be hopeful that eventually there will be forgiveness

The task in this final stage – following any kind of loss or bereavement – is investing energy in new ways of living and in different activities. If a carer has stayed close to the grieving person, they will recognise hope in those small changes. Perhaps a decision to go on holiday with a friend, join a club or adopt a new routine: 'I think I'll do that'; 'I've been wondering about this ...'

It may be something very small but it will signify the beginning of adjustment; a redefinition of self and environment and the recognition of renewed purpose in life. It's at this point that it can often be helpful to explore just a few options for life ahead.

There will be a gradual letting go of an old identity because there is an acceptance that the old identity needs to change: 'Who am I now?'; 'What does life mean to me now?'; 'What next?'

However positive those steps, there will be some ambivalence and guilt at this stage. Guilt, because the one who has died is no longer always the main focus. Going to the grave each week is no longer a priority. There are mixed feelings about moving on to something new: 'Am I betraying him/her?'; 'Am I forgetting him/her?' But the grief is mastered, not by ceasing to love that person but by taking what was fundamentally important in that relationship and reshaping it so that it is still cherished and precious but has been reformed internally as part of our being. Going on independently means 'detaching' from that former relationship by assimilating it as part of our life experience and *moving on*, carrying it with us in a different and no less precious way.

Gradually, a new sense of meaning and necessary purpose comes to the fore. The bereaved person will be more hopeful, calmer and begin to find meaning in life and acceptance of what's happened.

One of the early signs of recovery is the recognition by the bereaved that their emotional resources are available for others. Gradually, rather than saying, 'It's like this for me', they more often say, 'How is it for them?' and increasingly, 'I know – a little – about how it is for them.' There is a growing empathy whatever their painful situation because 'I've been there too.'

New skills, interests, responsibilities and social confidence begin to emerge. Normal eating, energy and sleeping patterns return. The bereavement experience gradually gains perspective with the recognition that the time will come when grief isn't the only thing in life, that it will not always be the main focus of the day.

Grieving at the wrong pace

Sometimes, the bereaved person will go into this last stage prematurely.

If someone has lost a partner they can enter into the euphoria of a new relationship too quickly and bypass much of the grieving process only to encounter it later.

That may not only happen in a relationship, but through a new job, a grandchild, a new home. A classic statement might be, 'I can focus on this now, it can get me through.' But it doesn't. It merely masks or buries an important part of the grieving process, denying a stage that needs to be walked through. Diana's mother was widowed at thirty, with two tiny children. She had to make a life for them and this left no time for personal grief. It was many years before she acknowledged personal loss.

Sometimes it can be many months, even years, after a loss that the bereaved person begins to slide back into the phase they missed. They haven't necessarily gone backwards, but they are experiencing what needs to be experienced as part of readjustment. Grief from divorce might also resurface in a second marriage if it has not been fully addressed.

The bereaved person may also introduce changes into their life too quickly in *trying* to accept their loss: 'I've got to make a new life for myself!'; 'I must make a fresh start.' There is a sense of wanting to get to the readjustment stage in an attempt to avoid the pain and agony of the despair phase.

Carers may not be able to give direct advice, but can gently discourage the bereaved person from making major life changes in the early days: moving house, moving in with family, beginning a new relationship, or changing jobs. Even quickly disposing of the dead person's belongings can be a way of not addressing the issues, preferring to brush them (or throw them) away. Any changes – and there will inevitably be changes – should be gradual, thoughtful and considered.

Some people will not grieve fully until the end of their lives. It is possible for someone to live their whole life in denial, particularly after a traumatic shock. They may need permission to go through the stage they have missed in a safe place with specialist help.

Generally, however, the process of readjustment continues indefinitely. The bereaved person will let go and remember, grow and learn.

At this stage, some Christians will not just 'hang on' to their faith but will find renewed meaning and relevance in it. Coming face to face with issues of eternity and mortality may help them to gain a new perspective on life and a new hope for beyond death. Often faith becomes deeper, more real and more grounded as we discover that our faith is not just a faith of fine words. It has been tested, it has sustained us and there is recognition that it will continue to sustain. That God really *is* faithful. The bereavement journey can lead us to thirst for a deeper relationship with God – and He will respond to that need.

The working journey that is bereavement can never be predicted because it depends on so many factors: the relationship between the bereaved and the one they have lost; the circumstances of the loss; their life, environment and family situation; and the inner resources – emotional and spiritual – that the individual brings to the task. Most will, however, finish the journey. Battered, bruised, but often strangely blessed. It is a journey that will often be relived; the bereaved may even re-travel parts of it many times over. But the large part of the journey will – eventually – be at an end.

PERSONAL REFLECTION

- Look back at a bereavement journey that you have experienced (or are experiencing) – either personally or in supporting someone else.
- Draw a diagram or write a piece of prose that describes that journey.
- Think about the beginning, the 'landscape' which was travelled through, the travelling 'companions' who helped on that journey, the tasks which needed to be done, the delays and the difficulties. Use as many journey metaphors as you can to shape a picture of that experience.

What does that exercise teach you about the bereavement journey?

How might you use it to help others as they embark on their own journey?

CHAPTER FOUR

SHARING THE JOURNEY

The bereavement journey can be a lonely and bewildering one. If carers can accompany people on their pathway of grief they will have offered more than help or support – they will have given companionship in suffering.

If they have known grief and loss themselves, carers might find it helpful to take much of their motivation and inspiration from the apostle Paul's beautiful words:

> Praise be to the God and Father of our Lord Jesus Christ, the Father of compassion and the God of all comfort, who comforts us in all our troubles, so that we can comfort those in any trouble with the comfort we ourselves have received from God. For just as the sufferings of Christ flow over into our lives, so also through Christ our comfort overflows. (2 Cor. 1:3–5)

Whether carers are the companion of a bereaved person they know well – a family member or friend, perhaps – or are entering the fragmented life of someone they have never met before, the qualities needed and the priorities for care will be the same.

THE QUALITIES OF AN EFFECTIVE CARER

Caring for the bereaved begins with the carer's attitude: an attitude of acceptance, tenderness and love.

Susan Lenzkes captures this beautifully when she writes:

The measure of loss you are experiencing
Is beyond my emotional comprehension.
Yet I ache with you and long to lift your load,
Even while knowing that you alone must carry
One grief at a time to the God of all comfort.
How I pray that He will lead you daily
To the storehouse of His grace, compassion and healing.
And on that day when I need help through grief's dark night,
I pray that you will grant me
The tender gift of you.[1]

Those are biblical attitudes and we can specifically trace their roots in both the Old and New Testaments.

From the very beginning, people must ensure that they are caring with the right motives (1 Cor. 4:5), not to meet their own needs or to improve standing or worth in the eyes of others.

The care and approach must be genuine and sincere (Rom. 12:9), free from hypocrisy and criticism. In humility (Phil. 2:3) carers should show unconditional acceptance not only of the person they are caring for but of their often overwhelming or unexpected feelings. Part of the role is to provide a safe place for those feelings to be expressed. A safe place means a confidential place, a non-judgmental place and one filled with tenderness.

Carers should avoid platitudes, 'sticking plaster' Bible verses and easy answers, and accept – and when necessary express – their own limitations in the caring relationship. We can never be all things to all people, or expect every word we utter to be timely or even tactful! We will sometimes make mistakes. Neither can anyone say, 'I know exactly how you feel.' Quite simply we do not. Even the person 'feeling' doesn't know 'exactly' how they feel – so how could the carer?

Empathy means those that care must ask: 'If I were in their shoes how might I feel and react?'; 'What might I need?'; 'How would I like to be cared for?' Carers may not always get the answers right – but can check them with the one they are caring for.

Empathy literally means to suffer from within. It communicates a deep desire to truly understand and to experience the suffering of the other.

Jesus modelled empathy on so many occasions. When He spoke to the widow of Nain before raising her son to life, we are told: 'When the Lord saw her, his heart went out to her … ' (Luke 7:13). Jesus put Himself in her situation and felt her grief through her.

That's what having empathy for the bereaved really involves. But it begins with listening to their story.

THE IMPORTANCE OF BEING HEARD

Each of us has a story we long to tell – our own story. Our experience of grief is a necessary chapter.

Give sorrow words.
The grief that does not speak
whispers the o'er fraught heart,
and bids it break.

William Shakespeare (*Macbeth*)

Shakespeare was right – it is important that we give voice to our grief and sorrow.

If somebody is in distress they need to be heard. To hear we must *be there*. To be there alongside one who is grieving is the most important part of 'hearing' their experience – even when they don't say a word. Being there sends the message, 'I am here for you. I am with you in your suffering.'

A listening ear – more than wise words – is the greatest gift anyone can give the bereaved. Just being alongside, sharing their pain, listening to their heart is often all they need – even all they can bear. Their main need 'is warmth, not words'[2]. To listen, we need to concentrate fully on the other person, tune ourselves in to their needs. We must, for a time, forget our own concerns, what we will say next, or what we have to do later. If the bereaved are important enough to us, they are important enough to give our whole attention. Hearing is more than the physical process of listening – it is an activity that involves our minds, emotions and bodies – as well as our ears.

For those who are listening, it is often helpful to reflect back what has been said in simple sentences and phrases. To repeat what has been said, to remember detail and nuance to show we understand and to build a genuine empathetic connection. We do not directly give the words to those expressing their grief, because to do so is an imposition which starves the bereaved of expression. But in reflecting the words they *have* been able to say, the carer may help them to say more.

Sometimes people in distress are unable find the words to express how they are feeling. Then, and only then, the carer may listen to their intent and tentatively make suggestions – without assumption – that may help them find those lost words.

Silence may communicate more than words. Often, we will need to learn to tolerate those silences and recognise them as an important part of the communication of grief. Pain is often a language without words. It will usually remain untouched by words, but it may be soothed by silence.

As carers listen to the bereaved and pray silently, they can ask for the Holy Spirit to help them hear, interpret and discern the heart of the one they are beside. Non-verbal clues, body language, stance and use of hands – wringing them or using them to shield the face – all communicate feelings which the carer might help to interpret. Often men are better at expressing and interpreting feelings through body language than through words, whereas women are more responsive to, and inclined to use, touch.

If we take our lead from the one we are listening to rather than from our need to say something we will be better companions.

MEETING THE NEED FOR TOUCH

Whilst gesture and touch can be used effectively to show concern and support, we must always ask permission to touch the one who is bereaved – and do so sensitively. Touch is not always appropriate, or wanted, and is open to misinterpretation. Respecting the boundaries set by the bereaved gives them security. But our expression and interactive and responsive body language can often communicate the emotional oneness of empathy when used appropriately and with care.

Diana shares a light-hearted story which illustrates the way in which the person who is bereaved often sets his or her own boundaries:

> When I was first bereaved I was allowing myself to cry because through my training as a bereavement counsellor I had understood that to be helpful. Male friends I knew from the bowls group would come to say how sorry they were – and everyone got a soggy hug!
>
> I would cry on their shoulders! I went round to all their wives afterwards to apologise: 'I'm ever so sorry but that was what I needed at the time.' It became a joke: 'Don't go and see Di, she'll give you a soggy kiss and a hug!'

But Diana identified what she needed at the time – and her friends obliged!

She adds, 'If somebody had pushed me off I would have found that difficult. Fortunately they were all quite good so we got through that one!'

The key is to develop an awareness of the needs of the bereaved, to help them express those needs and to meet them appropriately – even if that involves a soggy hug.

A MODEL OF CARE: FIRST THINGS

As companions on the bereavement journey, we know that we want to care for the bereaved. But what shape and purpose does that caring take? And how do we know we are meeting needs?

Our aim will be two-fold:

- To help people find and experience God's love in the midst of loss.
- To provide care and comfort through appropriate bereavement support.

We meet those aims when we:

- Provide individual care and contact which reflects our values and respects those of the one we care for.
- Build a network of support through friends, neighbours or a bereavement care team which utilises gifts and experience to meet immediate practical needs.

And most importantly when we:

- Reflect our love for God and for others with a servant heart which shares their suffering and walks alongside them on their bereavement journey.

To share that walk, we need to understand loss, the impact it has, the needs it creates, and the qualities we need to meet the needs of a bereavement situation.

THE IMMEDIATE IMPACT AND NEEDS OF LOSS

Death, bereavement and loss impact a family heavily, disturbing the emotional, physical and social state of each member and the family as a unit. Individuals will doubt their ability to cope and to move on and even simple and immediate practicalities will often be beyond their capabilities for a time. Whether the family have been prepared for death or divorce makes little difference. Shock and bewilderment are no respecters of preparedness.

Where a death is concerned, part of our role as carers will be to assess immediate practical and mid-term needs, and to identify a primary network of support.

Hospitals, residential homes and hospices follow recognised procedures when a death occurs (see, 'What to do When Someone Dies' Appendix 1) and will advise families of what to do next. Church ministers and GPs also offer much-needed guidance and support of relatives and friends in dealing with immediate needs. Funeral service representatives and undertakers will take responsibility for the physical requirements surrounding the deceased and in planning funerals and cremation services and will guide the bereaved person through.

But there will be considerations for which the bereaved will probably want – or need – to take responsibility.

When a funeral is arranged, questions which may have future impact on the grieving process have to be gently asked. 'What about flowers?', 'What sort of coffin?' and most importantly, 'Do you want to see the body?'

Seeing – or not seeing – the body of the one who has died is very important for some people, serving to 'prove' that the person has actually died. Others prefer to remember their relative or friend as they were alive – talking and laughing and being themselves.

It is a personal choice. There is no right and wrong way, although there is some suggestion that it is easier to 'let go' if the bereaved has been able to see the body, especially if it's a little child.

When a baby is stillborn or dies in the first days and weeks of life, it often helps the grieving process to be able to say a proper goodbye. It is part of the grieving ritual that is now widely recognised. Hospitals will usually encourage a small ritual and parents will be helped and supported in that process by the Spiritual Care Team or chaplain.

In the early stages of grief, help may be needed in completing the necessary paperwork: registering deaths, going to the bank, looking at financial documentation, listing all the things that need to be changed. Who should be informed? Where is the address book with the people who need to be contacted? What about announcing the death? An obituary? What about benefits? Access to bank accounts?

Some of those necessary tasks can be complicated and easily overlooked in the confusion and bewilderment that follows a death. The bereaved will not necessarily think of everything, will forget previously familiar details and will not always know where important papers, bank details and legal documents are kept. The smallest tasks can seem insurmountable. Consequently, support with such practicalities in the early stages is very helpful. Just someone being with them, going with them as tasks are performed, can be reassuring.

There may be sensitive – or even hidden – personal issues to face: an unknown relationship perhaps, or an unacknowledged gay partnership. Will the family acknowledge that relationship or accept the partner at the funeral? Such questions and dilemmas are part of the untidy business of death and bereavement. If we can help guide a healthy response and resolution we will be helping to move the grieving person on in their journey.

DAY-TO-DAY PRACTICALITIES

Everyday life goes on – even when that very fact seems illogical to the bereaved. There is still a need to attend to day-to-day practicalities: grocery shopping, meals, washing and ironing, housework, lifts to and fro, meetings with solicitors, accountants, and all the running of necessary errands.

We must be careful not to take control. The bereaved will already feel as if they have lost control of life – that life has 'turned on its head'. Their accomplishing small tasks can give back a little of that control. Even when we are offered the inevitable cup of tea when we visit, we should let the bereaved make it and not deny them the right to do what they can themselves.

Neither should we physically remove them from their situation or environment lightly. Taking over – 'Stay with us and you'll be fine' – is not helpful in those early days. The bereaved will still have to go back to their home, to the emptiness and the loss, and the carer's apparent kindness will only delay the inevitable. For many, going back to the empty house is the hardest thing to do. Sometimes a temporary move will be unavoidable for the sake of immediate care. But taking someone out of their situation doesn't help the grieving process. It may even trigger a stage of denial. Real life will – and must – always beckon 'back there' in their own home.

ASSESSING THE NEEDS

Carers will not be able to offer appropriate help and support beyond the immediate practicalities until they can effectively and specifically assess the needs of the person they are supporting.

They might do that by:

- Considering the bereaved person's ability to communicate their grief.
- Identifying current levels of practical support.
- Identifying friends, key family members and a wider current support network.
- Assessing their level of physical care and general health, including sleep patterns and drug and alcohol use.
- Identifying financial and housing concerns.
- Assessing their emotional and mental health needs – anxiety, depression, anger, guilt.
- Identifying any activities outside the home which may offer the means to 'outward' progress – work, clubs, activities, travel, voluntary work.

This checklist looks at these assessments in more detail.

1. Does the person appear able to:
   - ☐ Accept help?
   - ☐ Express freely what they feel?
   - ☐ Cope with the initial numbness of grief?
   - ☐ Shed tears and express their emotion?

2. Can you identify that the person has adequate support? (These questions may help.)
   - ☐ Who would care for their home or car if they were out of town for a while?
   - ☐ If they are in work, with whom do they talk to most about work-related matters?

☐ Who, if anyone, has helped with household tasks in the last three months?
☐ Who do they see as their friends?
☐ With whom do they talk about their hobbies and interests?
☐ Who is their 'closest friend'?
☐ With whom do they talk about their personal worries?
☐ Whose advice do they consider in making important decisions?
☐ From whom (if they could) would they borrow a large sum of money?
☐ Who are the adults who live in the same house?
☐ Are their church and minister/pastor supportive?

3. Is the person:
   ☐ Eating regularly? (appetite/weight gain/loss)
   ☐ Sleeping adequately?
   ☐ Waking at a particular time each night?
   ☐ Experiencing bad dreams?
   ☐ Complaining of physical symptoms? (In need of medical care?)
   ☐ Experiencing fatigue/lack of energy?
   ☐ Taking drugs?
   ☐ Drinking alcohol in excess?

4. Has the person any:
   ☐ Financial worries?
   ☐ Housing problems?
   ☐ Loss of status?

5. Is the person showing signs of excess:
   - ☐ Guilt?
   - ☐ Anger?
   - ☐ Isolation?
   - ☐ Activity?
   - ☐ Inertia and unwillingness to do things?
   - ☐ Anxiety?
   - ☐ Sense of personal worthlessness?
   - ☐ Fear about their future and their ability to cope?
   - ☐ Suicidal tendencies (expressed directly or indirectly)?

6. Is the person engaging in any:
   - ☐ Activities?
   - ☐ Voluntary work?
   - ☐ Full/part-time work?
   - ☐ Leisure/travel?
   - ☐ Daily outings, etc

NETWORK OF SUPPORT

Once the immediate personal needs of the bereaved have been identified, we can consider how to meet them in the 'responsive' context of a wider support network.

Those networks will spiral outwards through a primary network (friends, neighbours, relatives and workmates) to informal helpers (neighbourhood care schemes, youth club, playgroup, playground 'mums', the lady in the local post office) to formal help (hospital and social services, education, Primary Health Care, Cruse and Bereavement Services).

To identify that network, we as carers need to ask – directly or otherwise – the following questions: Who are the bereaved's closest friends? Who do they confide in? Which friends and neighbours do they meet on a daily basis? Which family members visit regularly? What about work colleagues and friends? Fellow club and society members? GP, hospital links and counselling services?

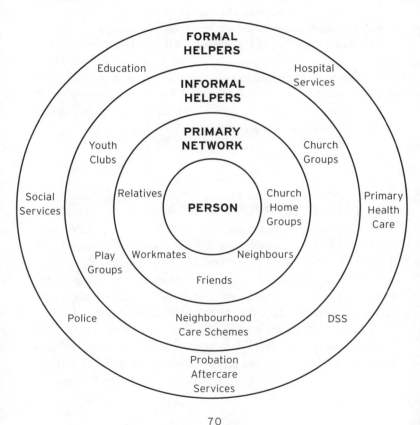

Our understanding, as carers, of existing support networks and the meaning and value they have to the bereaved person will help us to help the bereaved identify where the best, most reliable and most consistent sources of support may be found. We can then begin to arrange that practical help and support to meet both immediate and long-term needs.

Church fellowships often find it useful to form a permanent bereavement response group as part of a church pastoral team. It enables that team to be better prepared to give help and support when it is needed and to quickly identify a network for bereavement support in the early stages.

For a bereaved person to complete every step of the grieving process takes courage, openness, self-awareness and support from a wide and caring network. But members of that caring network also need to take care of themselves.

TAKING CARE OF THE CARERS

Caring for the bereaved is emotionally and physically exhausting. There is a need to keep an eye on carers' own emotional and physical balance as they care.

The oxygen mask principle reminds us of that need. It is illustrated on board a plane by the instruction given by the cabin crew to always put on our own oxygen mask before helping others to attach theirs. If our own needs are not addressed we will not be able to help effectively.

It can be difficult to emotionally disconnect from the needs of others. If we offer to share pain and suffering, we will not do so genuinely without feeling a certain amount of that pain ourselves. It goes with the territory. So before we choose to embark on what is, by necessity, long-term care of the bereaved, we must acknowledge the demands and sacrifices we may be asked to make along the way.

There are two main dangers which must be avoided: dependency and burnout.

Dependency

Our aim in supporting and helping the bereaved is for them to gradually return to a 'normal' life. Too much regular or lengthy contact, promises easily made – perhaps to fetch shopping every day – or giving inordinate amounts of time in help and support, may all encourage an unhealthy dependency. Especially if we become a substitute for the one who has died who perhaps did those things so dependably. To increase the independence and recovery of the bereaved person, we must know when to say a gentle but firm 'No'. To skilfully and gradually decrease the level of practical help as independence returns and to increase the emotional distance. If we can encourage a gradual 'letting go' of outside help and support we will be helping to build recovery and independence.

Someone can still be there, still offer company and care, but on shared terms. We may even need to ask ourselves, 'Who is this supporting: the bereaved or the carer's need to be needed?'

Burnout

If all our time, as carers, is invested in caring for others we will neglect our own health and well-being. 'Just this once' or 'It's only for now' can gradually chip away at reserves of emotional, spiritual and physical strength until we are in danger of exhaustion, stress-related illness or depression.

Jesus modelled 'time out' (Mark 1:35). If He needed time to rest and recuperate after meeting the needs of others – how much more do we?

It may be up to one carer to spot the dependency or burnout in the life of another. Often we cannot see the danger signs in the midst of the busyness of caring. We may need to look out for each other in order to look out for the bereaved.

PERSONAL REFLECTION

- Think about a time when you have been well cared for.
- What did you value most? What was less helpful?
- How can you use your own experience of practical care to increase your empathy – and to identify an appropriate network of care for those you serve?

PRAYER

Father, don't let me neglect what my head says about caring in following what I know my heart says. Amen.

CHAPTER FIVE

WHEN THE JOURNEY IS MORE THAN DIFFICULT

What about bereavement that is particularly prolonged, difficult or complicated? When the pain is increased in severity because of tragic circumstances or trauma? When a child dies or a partner is murdered? When a family of small children are left without a loving father? And how can we help, as carers, in these situations? We may find we simply can't. However, it is important for the bereaved to be directed safely to someone whose professional expertise and experience *will* help. Then we can take our lead from the professional advice regarding support and just – as ever – *be there.*

As carers we may recognise clear signs when grief is complicated or abnormal.

FEATURES OF COMPLICATED AND ABNORMAL GRIEF

If there is no sign at all – however small – of moving on with the grieving process after six months to a year there may be some cause for concern. The bereaved person may need specialist help to enable them to make progress.

Abnormal and complicated grief both take many forms, but can generally be recognised as:

- Delayed grief
- Absent or inhibited grief
- Chronic grief

• *Delayed grief*

Delayed grief – a form of complicated grief[1]– may be triggered at a later date by another loss. That grief may have been buried because it had earlier been denied.

Often a bereaved person will have become 'stuck' in a particular stage of grief, by certain factors. Or, a complication will be triggered by a simple incident – perhaps the death of a pet or of someone they didn't know well. Perhaps this was why the death of Diana, Princess of Wales was so significant for so many. It gave an outlet for the buried grief so many felt and an impersonal – indeed a national – setting in which it could be expressed.

A simple trigger of this type, sometimes many years after the first bereavement, will take the bereaved back to that earlier loss and they will find themselves needing to work through that grief once more. That may not necessarily mean that they have to return to the very beginning of the bereavement journey – but that steps will need to be retraced so that parts of the journey can be more effectively travelled.

A delayed reaction of grief or projection of one grief onto another grief may be a healthy thing if it can be worked – and walked – through, once more.

• *Absent or inhibited grief*
Absent or inhibited grief may appear as a stoic refusal to show emotion or to be affected by a loss. The bereaved person may carry on with practical tasks to do with the death – or in the case of divorce, the departure – of a loved one without showing any apparent sense of loss or outward grief. The business of caring for a young family or elderly parent, for example, may not give time to grieve. A carer may wait for the time for them to express emotion – but that 'time' may never come.

These responses are often the result of denial or avoidance. Denial is a self-protective mechanism that the bereaved person is not always aware of. Avoidance similarly preoccupies the mind so that it does not have to face the pain involved: 'I must get on with life' often hides an avoidance of grief.

Past emotional deprivation may also leave a bereaved person without the emotional resources for release and expression. The bereaved may never have been allowed to cry because of their culture or upbringing. If tears were frowned upon in childhood or any show of emotion was discouraged, the expression of those emotions can be almost impossible. When a parent dies there can be an added complication of needing to express that emotion at the death of the very parent who had forbidden it. Help may be needed in finding other ways to express their grief. If inhibited grief continues for some time it can lead to major depression, and for that reason will require skilled help.

• *Chronic or unresolved grief*
Chronic or unresolved grief can continue for many years after a loss and may be indicative of a hidden or unexpressed motivation to continue grieving.

For the person who is grieving, reaching the end of that grieving process would signal their going back to a normal life. Yet a return to normal life is seen as not honouring the memory of the lost person.

The chronically bereaved person may constantly ruminate over the negative aspects of their loss, keep a bedroom as a 'shrine', or go over the loss and its detail repeatedly. Or they may respond after many months have passed as though the loss were only yesterday.

This is more likely to happen if the loss is untimely or the person who is missed has died young. It becomes genuinely difficult to 'let go' of that person.

It will not be helpful for people to be told, 'You must move on.' They simply don't feel able to. But a window of opportunity may arise in conversation where a carer can suggest that some benefit may be gained from someone with understanding who can offer specialist help where they are *now*. Once the bereaved has explored that place, moving on from it may be easier to consider.

There may be an exaggerated reaction of one or more of the features of normal grief: anger that becomes vindictive, excessive guilt, obsessive behaviour, psychosomatic symptoms or suicidal tendencies: 'They died, I deserve to die too', particularly if the person who was lost died as a result of a traumatic incident.

Survivor's guilt is a very real phenomenon.

There might also be a very real belief that because an incident or tragedy has happened once, it will happen again: a mother may not sleep when her baby sleeps for fear of losing them through 'cot death' as she had her first child.

Skilled counselling or cognitive therapy may be needed to gently guide the bereaved person back into normal thought processes and to help them to regain perspective – and hope.

TRAGIC DEATH

Of course, to most bereaved individuals, the death they are mourning *is* tragic – expected or otherwise. But most experts agree that the length and severity of mourning are inversely related to the expectation of death. A sudden tragedy involving a young person is the last thing we expect even if we dread it. Parents do not expect their children to die before them. There is something 'wrong' about the death of an innocent baby. The shock and numbness in this situation will be great and all-encompassing. It will probably last longer, be more likely to grow complicated or to become abnormal than the shock involved in the death of an elderly parent. That's not to minimise any loss – but there is a degree of difference.

Suicide, one of the most traumatic losses, produces particularly outstanding and prolonged grief often with considerable guilt and self-reproach attached: 'Why didn't I realise?'; 'I should have been there to stop him'; 'What did we not give her that she needed?'

In most cases, suicide is the result of psychiatric disease, severe depression or schizophrenia and although that does not relieve the trauma and pain in any significant way, it does have major implications for Christians.

Pablo Martinez, a medical doctor and psychiatrist, and Ali Hull, write:

> While it is true that lives belong to God and no one therefore has the right to take their own life ... our Lord will undoubtedly take into account that the decision was not taken in full conscience, but under the effects of the disorder. This fact brings forth a ray of new hope to relatives who are forced to live with the overwhelming despair.[2]

Grieving can also be very different for those who are caring for a loved one who is terminally ill. Those who are prepared for death begin their mourning long before that death occurs, sometimes with the acceptance or acknowledgement of a definite terminal diagnosis. They often begin a process of 'withdrawal' from the one who will die. As will the one who is dying. This emotional detachment may barely be conscious, but it begins to prepare the two or more who are parting for their mutual loss. It is a subconscious attempt to lessen the pain that will inevitably have to be faced.

Sometimes the process and daily demands of caring for a loved one who is terminally ill will 'sidetrack' that early phase of mourning. As a result, denial may be a distinct possibility, even in the face of approaching, inevitable death.

Sometimes those demands are so physically and emotionally exhausting that when death comes there can be a sense of relief that the suffering – and the demands of caring – are over. That 'relief' will interrupt the grieving process for a short time, but grieving will continue afterwards. It is as if a 'breather' has been given to enable the bereaved carer to gather strength to complete the work of grief and continue the bereavement journey.

LOSING A CHILD

There is no doubt that the loss of a child is one of the most intense and painful losses a human being can experience. There is a natural injustice in the death of a child. We are suddenly brought violently face to face with vulnerability in its most tragic form and with the fact that no guarantees were attached to this little one's life.

Biblically, Jacob's mourning for Joseph is a paradigm of this loss (Gen. 37:34–35; 42:36,38; 43:14). Jacob recognises that the loss will change him – for life. He knows that he will never be the same. Despite the fact that he is surrounded by family, one son is still lost to him.

Memories of the child who has died 'grow' with the family, alongside siblings and other families with children of the same age. Parents will watch the progress of friends' children and remember. They do not only feel bereaved, but cheated, not just of their joy at seeing their child but of that child's joy. Weddings, graduations and coming of age parties that are held years, even decades, after a death are as painful as the early days. There is the added poignant loss of 'what might have been'. The loss is a multiple and far-reaching one.

Losing a child involves loss of identity as a parent – even when other children survive. It is expressed as, 'I was a parent to *that* child – as well as these – but she is lost.' The child is part of each parent and that element of identity is lost too. It as if a part of the parent has died with the child.

A mother or father will feel that they should have been able to prevent the death. They will have always been able to keep their child safe, watch over them and 'kiss it better'. But suddenly a situation has arisen in which that is impossible. Inevitably there is a sense of responsibility and guilt – consciously or unconsciously.

The death of a child is the death of part of the family. The consequences are far-reaching – both in that family, the extended family and even in the surrounding community, members of which also mourn.

It can cause a crisis in the parents' relationship, as each will often express their grief differently and the two may find it hard to communicate together. Talking openly and honestly is essential, not just immediately after the death – but for ever. Prolonged parental grief may cause health problems or depression long-term. It can be difficult for mothers especially – although not exclusively – to 'let go' of the child they have given birth to and cared for. It was their 'duty' to give birth, not to relinquish them to death. Letting go of the grief can seem like a repeat of that relinquishment. Or even a repeat of what happened before the death, perhaps of 'letting them out of my sight'.

Losing a child may make it difficult for parents to relate to or care for other siblings, causing those siblings to feel rejected or guilty themselves. They, in turn, will often feel as if in some way they have caused the death of the brother or sister. They need reassurance, consistent company and attention from mum or dad, grandparents and trusted carers who know them well. They also need much honest, positive communication and frequent, consistent sharing of feelings between each other and within the family.

WHEN CHILDREN GRIEVE

If adults are grieving they can lack the energy or motivation to acknowledge the grief of the children around them. They may not have the ability – even for a time – to pay necessary attention to it. It is hard for adults to understand death from a child's perspective, to handle their grief or to know how to intervene in it when they are 'OK'. If they are in the throes of grief themselves, it can be impossible.

None of us has been 'taught' how to handle the grieving process, yet parents can feel that they should be able to teach their children – or at least be able to do something to protect them. But they can't. They may have to accept that the way they involve their children in their grief, and understand their own, will be necessarily incomplete or inappropriate at times, but that love and honesty will be the best tools they can use as they try.

It might help to have some understanding of the way in which children grieve:

• *Infants and toddlers*
Infants and toddlers up to the age of about two will suffer loss mainly as separation anxiety – especially if it is the mother who has died. Crying will, understandably, be the main expression. Recovery will often be achieved in a relatively short period by the secure and reliable warmth and closeness of another familiar person.

• *Children from three to seven*
Children from three to seven probably struggle most in terms of grief. They simply do not have the cognitive maturity and make-up to process or understand what is happening to them. They

find it difficult to express their feelings and the way in which they frequently confuse real-life and fantasy complicates matters further. They require clear explanation of what has happened through both description and experience. With much repetition and clarification in simple terms, understanding can be built piece by piece.

If death is expected, children in this age bracket will be helped by as much simple preparation for that death as is possible. The truth about death needs to be explained simply and gradually. Death must be referred to accurately and by its name – not as 'gone to sleep' or 'passed away' – and without an overload of information which may only confuse. Sometimes giving short pieces of information – single sentences – and responding to or inviting questions gives children space to deal with that information on their own terms and in their own time. They will often 'come back' for clarification: 'Did you say that …?', 'Is it …?', and ask questions to 'fill the gaps' in their understanding.

Children are often very much more accepting and 'matter-of-fact' about death than adults and are often able to see it as an inevitable part of life.

Experts suggest that children of this age should be given the option to see the body of the person who has died. We may find that thought alarming, but such an experience has less impact at this age than it does for adults, and may help them to understand that this is a natural way to say goodbye. Older children will usually refuse. Their intellects and emotions are developing and beginning to demonstrate adult traits which may make them think differently. But neither should ever be pressurised or coerced out of their reluctance.

Children at this age need to be clearly told that they are not responsible for the death – even if they don't ask the question that leads to that answer. Siblings can carry the burden for the death of a brother or sister for years, reluctant to voice their guilt to parents for fear of triggering memories and grief.

Signs of grief are not always obvious or 'by the book' at this age. Whilst we cannot put everything down to grief or allow children to be manipulative in a grieving situation, we have to be aware that certain types of behaviour may be an expression of the pain being felt. More than anything, grieving children at this age will need to feel safe, included, loved – and heard.

• *Children from about eight to eleven*
At this stage children will have similar needs to their younger counterparts, but they may need more time to be helped to clarify and voice their fears, especially about the death that they witness in other settings (even on TV and film) and about the security of the future. It is common for them to have an 'It happened before so it will happen again' attitude. To believe that if one parent has died, the other will die too. They will often find it difficult to let the surviving parent out of their sight – even to be left in the familiar and safe environment of school or Grandma's house. Diana remembers at eight waking in a panic to find her mother absent – she was only talking to a neighbour in the garden – but to Diana there was the subconscious fear that Mum had followed Dad in death.

Children may need to be helped to express their emotions – perhaps through art, drama or play activities, or simply through talking. Just having an adult around who is prepared to talk simply and wisely about the death whenever that subject is raised by the child can be immensely valuable.

At this age children will commonly express grief through physical symptoms: tummy-ache, headache, psychosomatic illnesses and anxieties, poor appetite and bed-wetting, can all be a physical manifestation of an emotional problem with grief.

It almost goes without saying, that if children have witnessed a difficult or violent death they will need specialist counselling, particularly to deal with the distressing visual memories. They will need to hear and see words and actions which demonstrate normality and hope.

The routines and 'always dos' of life before the bereavement can reinstate some of the security that was known before, and give an indication that life can – and will – go on.

• *Adolescents*
Adolescents will respond to death in much the same way as an adult. The most significant problem is the risk of extreme behaviour problems, substance misuse, self-harm and depression – all of which need specialist help. Alcohol, drug use, or extreme behaviour can be an expression of bereavement and an instinctive (often only short-term) coping mechanism: 'It blots out the pain.'

Drug and alcohol use in this situation may merely be reactive and 'quick fix'. It does not necessarily mean there is an addiction but it does need understanding and attention.

Adolescents are at a difficult period in their lives, when their need for independence is often counteracted by their lack of self-confidence and self-esteem. It can be particularly difficult for children who are about to leave home (for university for example) to be faced with the terminal illness or death of a parent or sibling.

Going away at this point can seem like desertion. Just when they are about to grasp their independence it is compromised in a tragic way. These young people may need particular care if they are to deal with their grief and make that transition – now or later – in a healthy and guilt-free way.

All grief and loss are abnormal or complicated to a greater or lesser degree: abnormal because life, not death, was God's original plan for us – and yet death is now part of life; complicated because we are fallen human beings with limited understanding who try to go it alone.

Our faith gives us a focus in the face of bereavement and loss, a way to express our pain and Someone to express it to, who can 'take it' in whichever form we might choose, and however loudly we might cry out in anger and despair. It may not always make that pain any easier to bear, but being heard may be the first step towards healing.

PERSONAL REFLECTION

- Locate news stories which point to the likelihood of a particularly difficult or complicated grief for those involved.
- As you read, turn your heart to God in prayer.
- These heartbreaking stories are not ignored by God. He weeps for his broken and fallen world.
- Notice the aspects of these lives that you particularly want to pray for. Might your desire to pray specifically, teach you something about your own gifts?

You might find it helpful to read Psalms 137 and 138.

CHAPTER SIX

REMEMBRANCE AND LAMENT

The bereaved do not – should not – forget those whom they have lost: an obvious statement perhaps, but one that words and actions do not always reflect as we interact with those who grieve.

We all too often find memories shared by the bereaved 'awkward', try to change the subject when loved ones' names are mentioned, and even avoid it altogether, skating round the reality of their previous existence as if it were a hole in the ice. Yet remembering the person who has died, or who has left a relationship, is an important part of the process of adjustment, of assimilating the lost relationship into a new identity and a new life.

Rituals of remembrance and incidental memories can have great significance and potential for healing.

FUNERALS AND FORMAL RITUAL OF GRIEVING

Every culture has some sort of grieving ritual, whether that is funeral processions and paid wailing mourners, separation from society for a specified number of days or months or wearing black for a specified amount of time. All – in their cultural setting – are considered respectful both of those who are grieving and those who have died. The Victorians, particularly, perfected mourning almost to an art form.

Today we have largely lost the ritual and even the indication or symbolism that signifies that someone is in mourning. That indication is largely limited to wearing black or dark clothes to funerals by tradition, sporting a black armband on the football pitch, lowering a flag or observing a two-minute silence as a mark of respect.

Our advanced society lives with a two-faced view of death. Whilst we so often value life lightly, taking it for granted, we still hold death as sacred. Memorials to the dead are as contemporary as they are traditional. They are merely given a contemporary context: Ground Zero in New York, trees planted in school grounds, poems to loved ones in newspaper obituary columns, memorial seats in parks and gardens or piles of flowers to mark the scenes of road accidents or bombings. They signify that we have a need to show that we have appreciated the person who was lost, that the death means something to us. The contemporary and spontaneous memorial has largely replaced the traditional and organised.

Christian funerals and thanksgiving services often discourage the dowdy. If such gatherings are seen as a celebration of life and a freeing by Christ from death, colour and light is deemed more appropriate, communicating something of the triumph over death. That doesn't lessen the impact of the suffering, the sadness or the loss, but it sets it in context.

We do, however, need to take care that in acknowledging the triumph (as in the case of Janey, see Chapter Three) we do not hurry away the sadness, bury it under busyness, or leave it prey to hijack by depression.

When we deny or hide the extent of our loss we lose the capacity to deal with what Eugene Peterson[1] calls the 'personal detail' and 'intimate feelings' associated with loss. The personal details associated with losing someone significant to our lives that are intimately linked with our own, and the intimate feelings in response to that event that are a very necessary part of being human.

We need to give time and space for those details and feelings to be addressed in the days after a death. Ritual and routine may give a secure framework in which to do so.

A funeral service, cremation or thanksgiving service offers the formal ritual needed in which 'goodbyes' can be said. It may not have always been possible either to say 'goodbye' before a person's death – or even beyond it. A death abroad or a death which follows trauma or accident, in which post-mortems or police investigations are necessary, may sweep the natural process of farewell to one side.

Sometimes the bereaved may just 'go through the motions', too numb, dazed or grief-stricken to say goodbye in their hearts. They may need help to facilitate that goodbye at a later date, perhaps with a short and simple 'funeral' or 'thanksgiving service' or a ritual that enables a letting go of a loved one. That short time of reflection need only be five minutes long, but it can be a necessary acknowledgement.

That need to 'let go' may be just as valuable when we are dealing with other losses. Those who are reluctantly divorced may need to let go, not only of the person they loved but of the future they had hoped for. Letting go in that context needs to include an acknowledgement that the hoped-for future has not gone, but is merely different.

Death often brings varying emotions and memories to the surface. The bereaved may recognise a need for forgiveness. They may need to forgive the person who has died or forgive themselves in relation to that person. Any unresolved conflict, guilt or regret will need to be brought out into the open and worked with, if grief is not to become complicated.

Forgiving ourselves is often the hardest type of forgiveness. But until we can do so we will be unable to fully accept God's forgiveness.

HELPING PEOPLE TO REMEMBER

Just as bereaved people do not forget, they do not really ever 'come to terms' with their loss. They simply learn to live with it. That may mean adjusting to a very different kind of life, but one in which they will still want to remember the one they have lost.

Sensitivity to individual needs is important. Some people may genuinely prefer not to mention their loved one, others will find it hurtful if people avoid talking about them or avoid using their name. Sometimes it's best to be asked: 'Do you mind if I talk about …?'

Very often, bereaved people will relish the opportunity to talk, not just about the death that is still so close, but about life before, even many years before. Talking – about the joys as well as the pain – can mean sharing in healing conversation. This may need to happen over and over again.

Wendy visited Ruth whom she knew and whose husband had died a year or so previously. Ruth had agreed to be interviewed, on tape, for a magazine feature on bereavement. Many tears were shed together during that meeting. But once the main part of the interview was completed, Ruth shared more reminiscences of Mark, the husband she missed so much. They ranged from the poignant to the hilarious until both Wendy and Ruth were laughing uproariously at Mark's antics and the shared memories of his sense of fun and the difference he had made to so many lives. As they parted, Ruth said, 'It is so good to laugh about him – there have been too many tears.' Ruth dates that conversation as a turning point in her bereavement journey. A conversation filled with tears, laughter and memories encouraged healing.

Birthdays and anniversaries can be almost unbearably difficult. In the first few years they are dreaded through every approaching day and just have to be 'got through'. Special occasions and family events can herald the return of pain and be devastating. Close family members may remember, but they may also forget even the date, apparently adding insult to injury. But as time passes, anniversaries can become a healthy way of remembering the now assimilated loss on one day, as part of a life that goes on beyond it and as such may be encouraged.

Rituals of remembrance can be valuable, and it may be especially helpful for something positive to be planned before the date concerned. Carers might also offer to be with the bereaved on that day, remembering that grief is unpredictable, however long it has been lived with. A visit to the grave with a wife whose husband has died, followed by a walk along the country lanes which had been so enjoyed by the two of them before his death, gives space to talk, to remember, to cry – and to laugh.

Philippa decided to plant a tree every year on the anniversary of her father's death. He supported The Woodland Trust and loved the Ashdown Forest near his home. Planting a tree seemed an appropriate way to both remember his love and life and to ensure that life was the focus. Philippa and her mother felt that the trees they planted would grow under the watchful eye of her children – her father's grandchildren – long into the future.

OBJECTS AND BELONGINGS

Those who are bereaved may develop considerable attachment to the belongings and objects associated with the person who has died. What is an empty, unused chair to others may be *their* chair – and they may not even want anyone else to sit in it. Arrangements of furniture and domestic routines can be preserved even though the person for whom they were designed is no longer there to appreciate them. Letting go of associations is part of letting go of the person. It takes time to do so. Similarly, the hurried disposal of personal belongings belonging to the one who has died in an attempt to 'get organised' or 'move on', should not be encouraged. Even when the bereaved person has parted with much they will be reminded by more that remains.

Diana recalls going up into the loft of her house with her son some time after her husband's death only to have memories triggered twice over. She had moved into the house just five days before her husband died, and they had carried so many memories with the toys and belongings they stored away:

Everything we took up there brought memories of laughter and the fun of the things we used to do together as a family – all the little things that came out, the toys from childhood. Some we discarded, some we kept. It took me years to actually clear that loft completely because they were precious things that had to be dealt with one at a time.

Disposal of belongings can take weeks or months, but phasing that process is an important part of the bereavement journey as those moments can be used positively to remember and cherish: 'Oh I remember when she wore that dress for the ball …' may begin a vital – and healing – bittersweet conversation. Take care not to clear too much too soon or memories may be thwarted.

THE RELATIONSHIP CONTINUES IN A NEW FORM

We have already mentioned that the relationship the bereaved have with the one they have lost continues in some measure. It should never become an unhealthy preoccupation, but that person has been, and remains, an important part of the bereaved person's life. Their relationship is reshaped, still cherished and precious, but assimilated internally. That relationship will still mould and influence who they are beyond its loss and it can be remembered and celebrated. The bereaved may have entered a new phase of life, but that doesn't mean that this special relationship from a former phase has lessened in importance. None of us wants to disregard years of relationships that have been important to our growth and development.

MEMORY TRIGGERS

Photographs and video film may remind us of loved ones painfully – and enjoyably. But, for the most part, we can prepare ourselves for those moments of mixed emotions.

When Wendy visited the children left behind by a friend who had died of cancer, the youngest daughter was keen to show her 'Mummy's Book'. It was filled with photographs of 'Mummy', Wendy's friend, at different stages of her life, before and after the children – and before and after cancer. She was mostly pictured full of life and joy and whilst it was sad and difficult to think that her laughter and smiles were no more, it was also a special moment to share memories of 'Mummy who is with Jesus now' with little Anna.

We can brace ourselves for those planned moments, but it is often the unexpected memory or circumstance that triggers poignant, painful moments of grief: the forgotten pullover at the back of a cupboard, a birthday card discarded in a drawer, the smell of a familiar perfume on someone else, handwriting on an envelope. If we can use those moments: 'Well, look at that,' rather than dismiss them: 'I can't think about that,' they can be helpful moments. Acknowledging the fact that 'This is precious – but difficult' can help us move beyond that moment rather than become frozen in it.

It is a clear sign that we are moving forward when we are able to acknowledge the negative as well as the positive in a 'trigger memory'.

Frances found that she would still buy her husband's favourite biscuits, even though she didn't like them very much. They were a 'habit trigger'. At first she couldn't bear to change her biscuit-buying habits. But eventually she thought, 'Why should I buy his biscuits ... I'd rather have mine!' She even imagined him teasing her for 'getting the fattening ones again!' Remembering – in tears and laughter – is important.

LAMENT

Over centuries grief has been expressed through lament. As carers, we would do well to encourage those who grieve to find their own way to follow that tradition.

Lament is an expression of grief: a song or poem expressing loss, a wail in words. Often, when we are grieving, the process of lament gives us a voice that we couldn't previously find. Poetry and song carries our emotions for us and expresses our grief in a more eloquent way. It draws from a deeper well of emotion and produces expressions far more precise than anything we might have been able to say in conversation. How and why does poetry do that?

One of the functions of poetry is to express emotion – fear, despair, anger and bewilderment – so it fits the grieving experience well, even when we merely read it. If, when we are bereaved, we find a poem, song or lament which expresses our innermost pain we latch onto it and make it our own. We find ourselves sharing the grief of the one who wrote the words. They somehow make our own grief easier to control. It can be 'boxed' safely in the words before so that we find them easier to handle.

There is also a mysterious and raw truth in poetry that we can't quite identify. It seems to transcend logic, reason and symptom. Lament – poetry of emotion in its most raw state – does so to the greatest extent.

Eugene Peterson writes:

Lament isn't an animal wail, an inarticulate howl. Lament notices and attends, savours and delights in details, images, relationships. Pain entered into, accepted and owned can become poetry. It's no less pain, but it's no longer ugly. Poetry is our most personal use of words; it's our way of entering experience, not just watching it happen to us, and inhabiting it as our home.[2]

King David knew the value of poetry and lament. 'A man after God's own heart', David was someone very much in touch with his emotions, a 'man of sorrow' who expressed those emotions honestly. The Psalms are full of his most honest cries to God. Their raw and heartfelt lines have been clung to by generations of readers unable to express the depths of their hearts, but who have found that David, in the Psalms, does it for them.

David also knew how to grieve. He wept for Bathsheba's child (2 Sam. 12) and grieved for Amnon and Absalom (2 Sam. 13; 18:32–19:4). But it is his lament over the deaths of Saul and Jonathan that encapsulates his grieving heart.

Eugene Peterson again, writes:

David's mighty lament over the deaths of Saul and Jonathan draws us into the depths of a healthy human spirit as it deals honestly and prayerfully with devastating loss and all its attendant emotions.[3]

David's lament for Saul and Jonathan may not dictate a 'model' for grief, but it does help us to understand the nature of loss. The lament – and its setting – offer us a biblical story which follows a pathway of grief and a poetic expression of its depths.

As we read both, we can follow much of the bereavement journey we have identified:

Shortly after Saul died, David returned to Ziklag from his rout of the Amalekites. Three days later a man showed up unannounced from Saul's army camp.

Disheveled and obviously in mourning, he fell to his knees in respect before David. David asked, 'What brings you here?'

He answered, 'I've just escaped from the camp of Israel.'

'So what happened?' said David. 'What's the news?'

He said, 'The Israelites have fled the battlefield, leaving a lot of their dead comrades behind. And Saul and his son Jonathan are dead.'

David pressed the young soldier for details: 'How do you know for sure that Saul and Jonathan are dead?'

'I just happened by Mount Gilboa and came on Saul, badly wounded and leaning on his spear, with enemy chariots and horsemen bearing down hard on him. He looked behind him, saw me, and called me to him. "Yes sir," I said, "at your service." He asked me who I was, and I told him, "I'm an Amalekite."

"Come here," he said, "and put me out of my misery. I'm nearly dead already, but my life hangs on."

'So I did what he asked – I killed him. I knew he wouldn't last much longer anyway. I removed his royal headband and bracelet, and have brought them to my master. Here they are.'

In lament, David ripped his clothes to ribbons. All the men with him did the same. They wept and fasted the rest of the day, grieving the death of Saul and his son Jonathan, and also the army of GOD and the nation Israel, victims in a failed battle.

Then David spoke to the young soldier who had brought the report: 'Who are you, anyway?'

'I'm from an immigrant family – an Amalekite.'

'Do you mean to say,' said David, 'that you weren't afraid to up and kill GOD's anointed king?' Right then he ordered one of his soldiers, 'Strike him dead!' The soldier struck him, and he died.

'You asked for it,' David told him. 'You sealed your death sentence when you said you killed GOD's anointed king.'

Then David sang his lament over Saul and his son Jonathan, and gave orders that everyone in Judah learn it by heart. Yes, it's even inscribed in The Book of Jashar.

Oh, oh Gazelles of Israel, struck down on your hills,
    the mighty warriors – fallen, fallen!
Don't announce it in the city of Gath,
    don't post the news in the streets of Ashkelon.
Don't give those coarse Philistine girls
    one more excuse for a drunken party!
No more dew or rain for you, hills of Gilboa,
    and not a drop from springs and wells,
For there the warriors' shields were dragged through the mud,
    Saul's shield left there to rot.

Jonathan's bow was bold –
    the bigger they were the harder they fell.
Saul's sword was fearless –
    once out of the scabbard, nothing could stop it.

Saul and Jonathan – beloved, beautiful!
    Together in life, together in death.
Swifter than plummeting eagles,
    stronger than proud lions.

Women of Israel, weep for Saul.
 He dressed you in finest cottons and silks,
 spared no expense in making you elegant.
The mighty warriors – fallen, fallen
 in the middle of the fight!
 Jonathan – struck down on your hills!

O my dear brother Jonathan,
 I'm crushed by your death.
Your friendship was a miracle-wonder,
 love far exceeding anything I've known –
 or ever hope to know.

The mighty warriors – fallen, fallen.
 And the arms of war broken to bits.
(2 Sam. 1, *The Message*)

If we 'read between the lines' of David's lament we can identify some of the key stages and needs of the bereavement journey.

Denial and disbelief are evident as David listens to the young soldier's account. He presses him for details, doubtless in order to try to uncover some inconsistency that will reveal the tale as an untruth. As he realises that this tragedy really has happened his reaction is harrowing. He gives voice to his feelings.

In verse 11 David shows *deep distress and bitterness with overwhelming consequences* as he and all his men tear their clothes in grief. David is *angered and outraged* in turn by what he has heard. First his anger erupts as irritation as he speaks to the young soldier with impatience and disregard: 'Who are you, anyway?' Then in disbelief and outrage he says, 'Do you mean to say that you weren't afraid to up and kill GOD's anointed king?'

Revenge takes hold as David decides that somebody must pay. The young soldier becomes the scapegoat, the one to blame, the person who just happened to be in the wrong place at the wrong time, as he hears those last words: 'Strike him dead!'

The young soldier takes the full force of David's *blame*. Someone had to be responsible. 'You asked for it,' David tells the soldier. 'You sealed your death sentence when you killed God's anointed king.' David *loses his perspective* and deceives himself into thinking that it was the soldier's own fault that he was killed. That he 'deserved' it.

As David pens his lament, he has finally accepted the finality of the deaths: 'Oh Gazelles of Israel, struck down on your hills, the mighty warriors – fallen, fallen!'

He reflects on the characters of Saul and Jonathan and praises them, *idealising* each of them and the relationships between them in an attempt to answer the question *'Why?'* and find meaning in their deaths: 'Saul and Jonathan – beloved, beautiful! Together in life, together in death. Swifter than plummeting eagles, stronger than proud lions.'

The *sharpness of loss* is reflected as David acknowledges the love and friendship of Jonathan and *remembers* their time together, *grieving openly* for his friend: 'My dear brother … I am crushed by your death, totally crushed.'

Perhaps surprisingly, he honours Saul, *finding reconciliation* in death. Despite the fact that Saul has been a sworn enemy, and has made David's life a misery for fifteen years, in retrospect he finds much to praise in this man – reflecting his generous heart.

Gone is the acrimony and battle between them. Saul hated

David – yet magnanimity pours through these words. This is reconciliation. David doesn't even say, 'You may have done that *but* I still love you.' There are no conditions. This is grace. He sees behind Saul's behaviour, his unreasonableness and his mental illness to the real heart of the man – and *forgives*.

There is a nobility in these words; they do not invoke pity, yet the lament itself draws deep into the well of David's feelings and he gives vent to them – albeit poetically.

Writing the lament was a way of marking and remembering the finality of the death of these two significant men in David's life – for generations. So important was it, that David gave orders that everyone in Judah should learn it by heart. David wanted his mourning to be shared. His apparently private mourning became public and universal.

Yet, loss is rarely private. It is public – even political. Lament, like that which followed the death of Diana, Princess of Wales, and the terrorist attacks of recent years, shapes culture.

David's lament was as much about the vitality and hope of life as the tragedy of death:

> David who lived so exuberantly also lamented fiercely. His exuberance and lamentation were aspects of the same life-orientation – life *matters*. David honoured human life – the sheer fact of human life – extravagantly. The depth of lamentation witnesses the extent of veneration.[4]

At the very end of his lament – at the beginning of 2 Samuel chapter 2 we read, 'After all this, David prayed' (*The Message*). Beyond the enormity of that initial grief, God became David's focus once more. He was still part of God's 'story'.

Peterson concludes:

> We're in a story in which everything eventually comes together, a narrative in which all the puzzling parts finally fit … but we mustn't attempt to get ahead of the plot, skip the hard parts, detour the disappointments. Lament – making the most of our loss without getting bogged down by it – is a primary way of staying in the story.[5]

Through bereavement we can help each other not to subdue or deny the pain of loss but embrace it as whole human beings. Human beings designed by God who may weep for a time but who will also laugh later as we have laughed before – even if that 'later' seems a long way off. In doing so we will find that the pain of loss does not diminish us, but that eventually we will find understanding in it. We may even find God in it.

PERSONAL REFLECTION

- Is there a piece of poetry or a song that for you encapsulates the experience of grief?
- What is it about that piece which gives such a vehicle for the emotions attendant on the bereavement journey?
- How might you explore the role that memories, poetry and lament play in the grieving process?

CHAPTER SEVEN

GOD'S LOVE IN BEREAVEMENT

The Bible assures us that we have God's presence and assurance in the midst of our suffering and that He knows and understands pain and grief. He watched His own son suffer and die and knows what it is to feel bereft.

Bishop James Jones writes:

> God is not a spectator of human suffering. In Jesus we meet the God who cries and suffers pain … Jesus sets the life of each of us in the context of eternity … to know God means that even in suffering there is blessing.[1]

But it is often a long journey from bereavement to the point where the bereaved can recognise that 'even in suffering there is blessing' or even until it is possible to recognise the full extent to which God's love is present in bereavement. Until that recognition occurs it may be up to carers to be the channel of that love with a compassionate heart and servant hands and feet.

DISCOVERING GOD'S LOVE FOR OURSELVES

Bereavement is a time when a consideration of God's love is very much on the agenda – whether the one who grieves recognises or acknowledges that fact or not. Any time of pain and trauma is fraught with protest and questions. We may cling to God or wish to push Him away.

Trauma brings out the most noble of human qualities – and the worst. Our most selfish and selfless acts often surprise even us when we are under pressure. War, disaster and crisis remind us almost daily that we live in a world where there is loss and hurt, tragedy and disaster. But disaster – personal or national – can lead to revival.

It can lead us to ponder our mortality, consider the meaning of life and take stock: 'There must be more than this!'; 'Is there a God? If there is, where is He in this?' and 'Where do I stand with God?'

Bereavement may be the only journey in life on which someone will consider life and faith issues. Carers, walking alongside the bereaved, will find that they are in a position not so much to 'evangelise' but to help the bereaved ask questions, reflect on their experience and move towards a search for answers and resolution. Even discovery.

Sometimes a bereavement experience pushes people away from God in anger. But that's OK. God can take it. He knows the root of that anger and pain and His shoulders are broad enough to carry it. The Psalms, as we have noted, are full of anger and bewilderment: a source of the most human and honest of prayers.

Bereavement may also cause those with faith to doubt. They may fear that they are losing their faith. But doubt is not the opposite of faith. It is part of it. To doubt, we must first have faith. Doubt causes us to look again at the basis of our faith, at our journey of faith so far, and where it might take us next. Taking a long hard look at doubt and faith during a time of crisis can often lead us to a re-evaluation and a fresh understanding of what it really means to follow Jesus. In fact, we may eventually come out of a crisis of faith stronger in that faith than when we went in.

For those *without* identifiable Christian beliefs, the adjustment or recovery stage of the bereavement journey often brings with it a recognition that there is a 'bigger picture' than just this life and that there is something more to be explored. That recognition can lead to an acknowledgement that we are created to have a longing for God and for Him to fill the God-shaped space within us, to meet us in the midst of our emptiness.

Such consideration highlights the question: 'What about somebody who dies without faith?' We will not always know the faith history even of those who are closest to us. Neither will we know how much a person may have been aware of God before death. But we can be reassured, or reassure the one who grieves, of God's love and mercy, remembering that God knows the story of our lives and the contents of our hearts. We cannot know whether a dying person's last moments were those in which they met God.

We do know as Christians that it is plain that we will not be with God in eternity if we have not acknowledged His Son (John 14:6) but He will continue to reach out for every one who is lost, until the last moment. We have to trust God utterly – and acknowledge that there may even be grief in the 'letting go' that such trust entails.

Jesus prayed for Himself, His disciples and all believers before He died (John 17). But His attitude to leaving His disciples and the earthly perspective He gave to eternal life remind us that the relationship we have with Him is a continual one, through life, until death and beyond it.

BEING THE CHANNEL OF GOD'S LOVE FOR OTHERS

The basis of our love for others is that God first loved us. Our love for Him is the motivation and inspiration for our love for others (Luke 10:25–37). Our compassion rooted in the compassion He shows us. Paul's beautiful words once again remind us:

> Praise be to the God and Father of our Lord Jesus Christ, the Father of compassion and the God of all comfort, who comforts us in all our troubles, so that we can comfort those in any trouble with the comfort we ourselves have received from God. For just as the sufferings of Christ flow over into our lives, so also through Christ our comfort overflows. (2 Cor. 1:3–5)

What a lovely picture 'overflowing comfort' gives! If carers are to be a channel of that 'overflowing comfort', they must first ensure that it will not be overwhelming! The bereaved can feel as if they have lost control of life and death. Even in the process of sharing love and compassion, control must not be take away from them.

When Shelley's husband died, her church fellowship went into action. They organised a rota for meals, shopping, housework and school runs. Shelley was, at first, grateful for their care. But within just a few days she felt overwhelmed to the extent that she felt that the steering wheel of her life was being controlled by others, just when she was trying to keep a grip on it herself.

Once her vulnerabilities were recognised, Shelley was given the support she needed through one person who co-ordinated the meeting of her practical needs and facilitated her gradual recovery. 'Overflowing comfort' should not be 'smothering love'.

There are very real practical ways in which people can show God's love in bereavement as individuals and as a church fellowship.

As an individual:

- Send a card or note containing just a few words and, if appropriate, mentioning something special we remember about the person who has died.

- Remember that it is not enough to say, 'If you need help, phone.' Most people won't. Individuals need to offer specific, consistent, relevant help – long-term. If a 'bereavement team' are co-ordinating a practical response, carers should do so via that team.

- Offer company – gently and sensitively – for tasks and errands which may not have been tackled alone before.

- Offer to drive (driving is often bewildering in the early stages), write essential letters or share necessary tasks.

- Remember that the bereavement journey is a long one and that many people not sharing that journey will 'forget': that is when individuals need to remember most.

- Be aware of anniversaries which may be approaching and ask what can be done to support the bereaved person – both immediately before, and through that day.

- Include the bereaved in family events, meals and outings when they feel able, and perhaps particularly in the later adjustment stage. Being alone does not mean *wanting* to be alone.

- Understanding that a hug or a gentle touch – with permission – may make all the difference. Some bereaved people may go for long periods without experiencing touch.

As a church fellowship:

- Consider establishing a 'bereavement team' to care for the bereaved in the church fellowship and community. If necessary, arrange 'skilled listener' and bereavement training.
- Be aware of the way in which some church traditions and routines may exclude or unintentionally hurt the bereaved: Mothering Sunday, baptisms and dedications, the announcement of subsequent deaths and funerals or 'family' events. It might sometimes be helpful to give 'warning' in advance. Not so that the bereaved person necessarily avoids an event, but so that they can be prepared.
- Include sermons and Bible studies in the church teaching plan that address issues involving death and bereavement to increase understanding, biblical knowledge and an eternal perspective on death.
- Consider ways to liaise with local bereavement groups, doctors' surgeries, hospices and hospitals to share expertise and support services. Not with the aim of 'evangelising' but of simply showing God's love.
- Hold a simple and reflective service of remembrance annually – perhaps in the difficult weeks approaching Christmas – for those who have recently been bereaved. Include candles of 'remembrance', space for thought and reflection and a message of hope. The fellowship may wish to ensure that support is available through skilled listeners for those who might need prayer,

listening or practical help afterwards.
- If the church arranges flowers regularly, allow those who are bereaved to commission or design flower arrangements in memory of those they have lost on key anniversaries.
- Consider holding a Christmas lunch for those who would otherwise be alone, or for those who find Christmas a particularly difficult time.

PUTTING THINGS RIGHT – THE IMPORTANCE OF FORGIVENESS

We are created for relationship both with God and with one another. God longs that our relationship be restored with Him and with each other. Even the hours, the moments, before death are not too late. Our God is a God of reconciliation and grace.

Diana shares the story of a woman who was aware that she was dying and said to her friend, a church leader, 'I really seem to have lost the presence of the Lord, and I can't get in touch with Him at all.' In response, her friend came alongside her and said, 'Look, I'm going to put a chair by your bed and I want you just to imagine that Jesus is sitting there. And I want you to talk to Him when you feel the need. Just respond to His presence next to you and try and talk to Him.' She agreed.

A few days later she died just a short time before her minister friend arrived to visit her. He asked the nurse, 'Did she die peacefully?' To which she replied, 'Very peacefully, yes. But there's one thing I don't understand. Just before she died she asked me to pull the chair closer to her bed so that she could hear.' The friend left reassured that she had indeed 'got in touch' with her Lord, and was now with Him.

God can work even in those last hours, minutes, seconds. He loves each and every one of His children and does not want a single one to be lost (Matt. 18:12–14).

If there have been breakdowns in relationship between family members or friends, a friend or other carer may be able to help people to put things right before death. If at all possible.

Unresolved conflict or tension, words regretted or words left unsaid can complicate the grieving process far beyond the death. Carers may be able to offer opportunities and space for reconciliation to happen, to urge both parties as a mediator, but a third party cannot force reconciliation. It may be that they can only pray into a situation and be a channel of God's love to others, gently urging the unforgiving to forgive, or the one still awaiting forgiveness to simply ask for it.

Forgiveness is a choice, not a feeling, but when the choice to forgive is made, release often follows close behind.

THE NEED FOR SPIRITUAL NOURISHMENT

The Bible clearly states that death is the enemy. God is concerned over the grief His children know, the suffering they endure, and weeps with us in it. But faith transforms that grief and the tears. It gives us the resources both for the work of grieving and the work of supporting those who grieve.

He equips us through:

- Prayer
- The Bible
- Worship

We often see those three 'disciplines' as a God-given framework within which to live and work as Christians. If we are bereaved, we may find it helpful to think in terms of those 'disciplines' as being rather more fluid. As such they nourish us as we live day to day; serve day to day, love day to day. They flow in and out of our relationships, our words, our greetings and departures, mixing and meeting and working together.

For carers, if we hope to support those who grieve with integrity and love and a spontaneous and genuine response, we will depend on each one, and the blending relationship between all three. They will sustain, inspire and guide us as we reach out to others at their lowest ebb and to carry the essence of the love of God into the lives of those who mourn, as God Himself reaches out to them.

Prayer

Prayer is simply drawing close to God, aligning our will with His, and bringing our lives and His plan for our lives together. It is communication as well as consultation. When we pray for others we bring them into the presence and oversight of God.

Sometimes, as carers sit and walk with those who grieve, they may need to silently pray for wisdom and discernment in a sensitive situation. The Holy Spirit (John 14:15–16) gives that discernment through prayer (1 Cor. 2:12–16), through His Word (Psa. 19:7) and through special insight. He even prays for us when we simply cannot find the words (Rom. 8:26–27).

When praying for and with the bereaved, it may often be necessary to take the lead from the bereaved person, asking permission to pray and keeping spoken prayers short, simple or even silent. Sometimes it helps to write down a short prayer to leave with those who are grieving to pray later, when they feel able, and as and when they wish.

Often people who are bereaved find comfort in familiar prayers and psalms – The Lord's Prayer or Psalm 23. A carer's role is to help the bereaved find a way of communicating with their God if they feel able to – sometimes writing a 'letter' helps – or to communicate on their behalf when they don't.

The Bible

The Bible illuminates. It sheds light on dark places (Psa. 119:105). No less so in the darkness of grief. It is filled with stories of loss and suffering which offer empathetic support and understanding in times of bereavement and give reassurance (2 Cor. 12:9) and hope (John 16:20).

It is not appropriate to quote large chunks of the Bible at those who are hurting, or to direct them to lengthy passages of prose that will 'help' them. What is needed at this time is a glimpse of God's Word that really does shine some light in the darkness: a verse or two of reassurance written on a card, a book of verses selected and compiled just for those who mourn, and again – a return to the familiar.

Margaret spent the days after her mother's death reading and re-reading Psalm 23, sometimes in fragments through tears, sometimes in entirety and with great hope. God's Word, wisely offered, can be light and strength in dark times.

Worship

To worship in the midst of pain is perhaps the most precious form of worship.

God acknowledges that worship as a 'sacrifice of praise'. The Psalms are full of such experiences. Psalm 42 is at the very margins of that experience – acknowledging grief but looking forward to praise. Psalm 102:1–11 acknowledges grief but clings to hope in God. So many psalms begin in despair but in the very process of honest worship from 'where I am' the heart is lifted and the psalm ends with praise (Psa. 57; 61; 71; 77). Psalms 137 and 138 are coupled together and show the long slow journey that is faith in bereavement. There is an acknowledgement in these words that despite the circumstances God *is* in control and is to be praised. Worship often moves us from doubt to faith, from mourning to joy: 'the oil of gladness instead of mourning, and a garment of praise instead of a spirit of despair' (Isa. 61:3).

How can the bereaved be encouraged to worship? Perhaps that is not for someone else to do. Worship may be almost impossible in the midst of grief. Celebration seems callous, joy unthinkable. Yet the Holy Spirit, in His gentleness, can use small moments to turn a grieving heart to Him. That moment might be in the recognition of the beauty of a flower, the acknowledgement and thankfulness for human love, gratefulness for the peace of sleep after sleeplessness.

Worship in this context may begin with thankfulness. God knows our hearts, especially when they are aching, and will discern and rejoice in the tiniest breath of praise.

JESUS AT THE TOMB OF LAZARUS: A MODEL OF GRIEVING, EMPATHY AND HOPE

Jesus asks where they have laid Lazarus.

'Come and see, Lord,' they replied.

Jesus wept.

Then the Jews said, 'See how he loved him!'

But some of them said, 'Could not he who opened the eyes of the blind man have kept this man from dying?'

Jesus, once more deeply moved, came to the tomb. It was a cave with a stone laid across the entrance. 'Take away the stone,' he said.

'But Lord,' said Martha, the sister of the dead man, 'by this time there is a bad odour, for he has been there four days.'

Then Jesus said, 'Did I not tell you that if you believed, you would see the glory of God?'

So they took away the stone. Then Jesus looked up and said, 'Father, I thank you that you have heard me. I knew that you always hear me, but I said this for the benefit of the people standing here, that they may believe that you sent me.'

When he had said this, Jesus called out in a loud voice, 'Lazarus, come out!' The dead man came out, his hands and feet wrapped with strips of linen, and a cloth around his face.

Jesus said to them, 'Take off the grave clothes and let him go.'

(John 11:34b–44)

Jesus arrives, apparently late, at the tomb of His dear friend Lazarus. The two sisters, in their grief, characterised by bewilderment and anger, demonstrate their faith in Jesus by saying: 'Lord, if you had been here ...'

But Jesus is in control. He knows what the outcome of this sad scene will be. He knows the higher broader plan that will be woven into this incident: a demonstration of victory over death through faith in Him. He reassures Martha that there is life after death. He asks her to affirm her faith – and then He visits the tomb.

To begin with, He grieves. Those two words, 'Jesus wept', perhaps tell us more about the compassion of Jesus than any others. He was grieving not only with and for, the sisters, but at the ugliness and futility of death: at the marring of His Father's design for life, and for the many who had already known its finality.

Even as Jesus grieves, His words and actions remind us what our attitude should be. Jesus was fully human – and fully God. This scene beautifully illustrates that fact. God is in control, yet He weeps the tears of human loss and compassion. And then He prays – and they wait.

There is so much waiting and empty silence in grief. It is filled with the mix of bitterness, pain, fragile hope and trust that Martha and Mary felt as they stood by the tomb, their eyes upon Jesus, heaviness and hope mingled uneasily in their hearts.

You can see the tomb of Lazarus in Bethany today. It is some distance underground. About twenty circular steps take you downwards to a series of small chambers, the last of which – the burial chamber – requires crawling under a ledge of rock on hands and knees to reach it.

Consequently, Lazarus' appearance would not have been instantaneous at Jesus' call to 'Come out'. It would have taken him some time to 'come to', to unwind the most restrictive cloths from his face and arms and legs, to raise himself stiff from the deepest of sleeps – death – to his feet. Then he would have had to crawl through a gap, stagger along the passageway and climb those twenty steps.

All the time the crowd outside would be waiting, hanging on to Jesus' words. Wondering, hoping beyond hope. Until at last there is a little shuffle and Lazarus appears, dazed, amazed, covering his eyes against the bright light of the day – and pandemonium of joy breaks loose! Grief is gone in a moment, and the power and love and victory of the One who gives us eternal life is demonstrated on earth.

Wow!

He weeps, He stands with us in grief, He waits with us – but He is in control. He has power over death and He has the gift of eternal life.

Perhaps the way those who care can best be the channel of God's love in bereavement is to 'mourn with those who mourn'. To help those of us who grieve express our anger, face our fear, find or affirm our faith (Rom. 12:15) and to 'wait' with us in the face of the tomb that is life, through all the wondering and the hoping, until that day when pandemonium and joy break loose and grief is gone in a moment.

In bereavement, as the bereaved or as carers, let us be reminded:

> If I stoop
> Into a dark tremendous sea of cloud, It is but for a time;
> I press God's lamp close to my breast
> Its splendour, soon or late will pierce the gloom; I shall emerge one day.

Robert Browning *(Paracelsus)*

APPENDIX 1

What to Do When Someone Dies

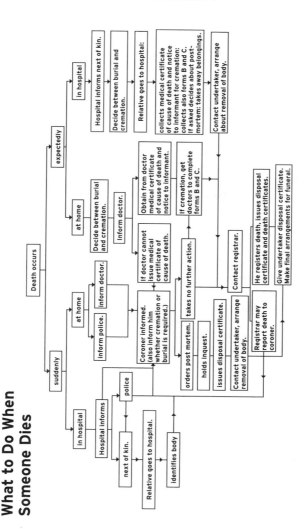

Taken from *Letting Go*, Ian Ainsworth-Smith and Peter Speck, SPCK. Printed with permission.

NOTES

INTRODUCTION
1. Pablo Martinez and Ali Hull, *Tracing the Rainbow* (Spring Harvest/ Authentic Media, Milton Keynes, 2004).

CHAPTER TWO
1. Gerald Sittser, *A Grace Disguised: How the Soul Grieves Through Loss*, quoted in John Ortberg, *The Life You've Always Wanted* (Zondervan, Grand Rapids 2003) p.211.
2. C.S. Lewis, *A Grief Observed* (Faber, London, 1976).

CHAPTER THREE
1. Penelope Lively, *Perfect Happiness* (Penguin, London, 1985).

CHAPTER FOUR
1. Susan Lenkzes, *When Life Takes What Matters* (DHP, Grand Rapids, 1999)
2. Pablo Martinez and Ali Hull, *Tracing the Rainbow* (Spring Harvest/ Authentic Media, Milton Keynes, 2004) p.60

CHAPTER FIVE
1. A detailed exploration of complicated grief can be found in J. William Worden's excellent book *Grief Counselling and Grief Therapy: a Handbook for Mental Health Practitioners* (Brunner-Routledge, part of Taylor-Francis, Basingstoke, 2003)
2. Pablo Martinez and Ali Hull, *Tracing the Rainbow* (Spring Harvest/ Authentic Media, Milton Keynes, 2004) p.15

CHAPTER SIX
1. Eugene Peterson, *Leap Over a Wall* (HarperCollins, Grand Rapids, 1997), p.120
2. Ibid, p.118
3. Ibid, p.115
4. Ibid, p.115
5. Ibid, p.121

CHAPTER SEVEN

1. James Jones, *People of the Blessing* (Bible Reading Fellowship, Oxford, 1998)

FURTHER READING

A Death in the Family (Lion Publishing, updated regularly).

All in the End is Harvest – An anthology for those who grieve, Ed Agnes Whittaker (Darton, Longman & Todd, 2001).

God of the Valley – A journey through grief, Steve Griffiths (Bible Reading Fellowship, Oxford, 2004).

Good Grief, Barbara Ward and Associates (Jessica Kingsley Publishers, London, 1995).

Grief Counselling and Grief Therapy: A handbook for mental health practitioners, J. William Worden (Brunner-Routledge, Basingstoke, 2003).

Letting Go: Care of the dying and bereaved, Peter Speck and Ian Ainsworth-Smith (SPCK, London, 1982).

On Death and Dying, Elisabeth Kubler-Ross (Tavistock, Basingstoke, 1969).

The Wheel of Life – A Memoir of Living and Dying (Bantam Books, London, 1997).

Tracing the Rainbow, Pablo Martinez and Ali Hull (Spring Harvest/ Authentic Media, Milton Keynes, 2004).

When Someone Very Special Dies, Marge Heegaard (Woodland Press, Chapmanville, WV). This is an excellent children's workbook.

Insight series

Handling issues that are feared, ignored or misunderstood.

Explore our full range of *Waverley Abbey Insight Series* books, courses and pamphlets.

BOOKS

Insight into Anxiety
by Clare Blake and Chris Ledger
ISBN: 978-1-85345-662-6

Insight into Self-Esteem
by Chris Ledger and Wendy Bray
ISBN: 978-1-85345-663-3

Insight into Depression
by Chris Ledger and Wendy Bray
ISBN: 978-1-85345-538-4

Insight into Stress
by Beverley Shepherd
ISBN: 978-1-85345-790-6

 **ALSO AVAILABLE AS EBOOK/KINDLE**

For a complete list of all titles available in this series, visit
www.cwr.org.uk/insight
Available online or from Christian bookshops.

COURSES

These invaluable teaching days are designed both for those who would like to come for their own benefit and for those who seek to support people facing particular issues.

For the latest course information and dates about CWR's one-day Insight seminars, visit **www.cwr.org.uk/courses**

PAMPHLETS

These short guides offer help in understanding and addressing problems effectively. They come in packs of 10 so you can always keep them handy to give to those affected.

Waverley Abbey Insight Pamphlet – Stress
ISBN: 978-1-85345-608-4

Waverley Abbey Insight Pamphlet – Depression
ISBN: 978-1-85345-609-1

Waverley Abbey Insight Pamphlet – Self-Esteem
ISBN: 978-1-85345-637-4

Waverley Abbey Insight Pamphlet – Anxiety
ISBN: 978-1-85345-641-1

Available online or from Christian bookshops.

STAY IN TOUCH
@CWRnews
www.cwr.org.uk/insight

Be encouraged and strengthened

Your Personal Encourager

Selwyn Hughes addresses 40 of life's most common issues, including fear, disappointment and bereavement, and applies Scripture to help readers see the way ahead.

Author: Selwyn Hughes

ISBN: 978-1-78259-579-3

What to Say When People Need Help

This useful guide contains many Scripture references that help equip readers to effectively address 36 frequently asked questions about issues such as depression, marriage and prayer.

Author: Selwyn Hughes

ISBN: 978-1-85345-514-8

For latest prices and to order visit **www.cwr.org.uk/store**
or call **01252 784700**
Also available in Christian bookshops.

Discover a biblical approach to caring for others

Caring and Counselling

Designed for those with an interest in counselling, this is an introduction to the Waverley Model of Counselling. First developed by Selwyn Hughes, the Waverley Model is based on a biblical perspective of what it means to be human, and why emotional and spiritual problems arise in people's lives.

Author: Ron Kallmier

ISBN: 978-1-85345-541-4

For latest prices and to order visit **www.cwr.org.uk/store** or call **01252 784700**

Also available in Christian bookshops.

Courses and seminars

Publishing and media

Waverley Abbey College

Conference facilities

Transforming lives

CWR's vision is to enable people to experience personal transformation through applying God's Word to their lives and relationships.

Our Bible-based training and resources help people around the world to:
• Grow in their walk with God
• Understand and apply Scripture to their lives
• Resource themselves and their church
• Develop pastoral care and counselling skills
• Train for leadership
• Strengthen relationships, marriage and family life and much more.

CWR Applying God's Word
to everyday life and relationships

CWR, Waverley Abbey House,
Waverley Lane, Farnham,
Surrey GU9 8EP, UK

Telephone: **+44 (0)1252 784700**
Email: **info@cwr.org.uk**
Website: **www.cwr.org.uk**

Registered Charity No. 294387
Company Registration No. 1990308

Our insightful writers provide daily Bible reading notes and other resources for all ages, and our experienced course designers and presenters have gained an international reputation for excellence and effectiveness.

CWR's Training and Conference Centres in Surrey and East Sussex, England, provide excellent facilities in idyllic settings – ideal for both learning and spiritual refreshment.